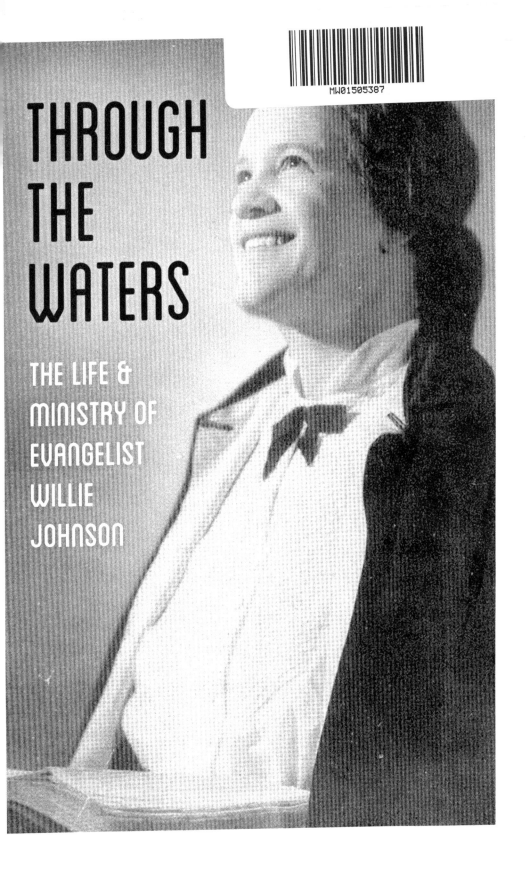

THROUGH THE WATERS

THE LIFE & MINISTRY OF EVANGELIST WILLIE JOHNSON

MW01505387

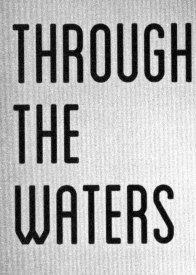

THROUGH THE WATERS

THE LIFE & MINISTRY OF EVANGELIST WILLIE JOHNSON

LORI WAGNER

ADVANCE PRAISE

"In her newest book, *Through the Waters*, Lori Wagner introduces readers to one of yesteryear's most dynamic Apostolic evangelists. When I was just a boy, Sister Willie Johnson held powerful revivals in my home church. I was nearly mesmerized by her anointing and genuine Apostolic ministry. I highly recommend this book. All Apostolic ministers need to meet Sister Willie, and this book provides you with a wonderful opportunity to do so."

—Jack Cunningham
 Virginia District Superintendent of the United Pentecostal Church International, Pastor, Bible Word, Chesapeake, Virginia

"If you are interested in knowing how to survive in the service of the King, *Through the Waters* is a must read. It will put steel in your backbone, great compassion in your heart, and this story will give wings to your faith. The life of Willie Johnson proved 'nothing is impossible with God.' Whether through fire or water, you can survive and do a monumental work for the Lord.

"This is an awesome work. Thank you, Lori."

—Edwin Harper
 Bishop, Apostolic Life Cathedral, Huntington, West Virginia

"In a time I'd like to label 'The Golden Era' of the Pentecostal Apostolic movement in North America, Willie Johnson was a biracial giantess. The 'apple of the eye' of Almighty God, she captivated the lives of many through the fulfillment of her holy purpose. Sister Willie was living proof that God would and could use the unlikeliest people to accomplish His great works, even in the face of racial upheaval and the evils of prejudice inflamed by cultural pressures and spirits of darkness. May this brilliant work speak to the racially sensitive culture of this era that God isn't limited by race; He's only limited by man's definition of it."

—Rico Smith

Founder, Rico Smith Ministries, Director of Youth Ministry, Pentecostal Assemblies of the World, Mississippi & Western Tennessee District

"Reading Lori Wagner's manuscript, *Through the Waters*, I found myself thinking about Luke, the writer of the third Gospel and Book of Acts. He was a second generation believer and so had to carefully assemble the story about Jesus from the stories of aging eyewitnesses. Many such stories had already been lost because those who would have told them had already fallen asleep in the Lord.

"Lori Wagner has labored under similar conditions. As with the Gospel of Luke, however, *Through the Waters* unfolds the story about the life and ministry of Willie Johnson in ways that bring to life that irrepressible wisdom and Holy Spirit anointed gift that those who knew her treasure so highly.

"This book is itself a gift. Without it, memories of this incredible woman might have continued to fade. Read with an open heart, the story of her life has so much to offer to an age like ours, which finds it all too easy to doubt that human beings can actually become saints — life-giving, through whom healing grace can yet move to empower us to, like them, to 'run all the way.'"

—Dan Scott

Senior Pastor, Christ Church Nashville, Nashville, Tennessee

"This book had to be written! It's a story that had to be told. *Through the Waters* is the amazing account of how far God will go to find one whom He had chosen 'from the foundation of the world,' as Sister Willie often preached. This book is the story of Willie Johnson, a handmaiden of the Lord, born under a cloud of social stigma and plucked from the misery of a coal camp in a hollow on the outskirts of Moundsville, West Virginia, to become one of the premiere evangelists of the post-Azusa Street Apostolic era. You will weep, you'll laugh, you will be inspired by the Willie Johnson story. As she sang; 'This is my story, this is my song, praising my Savior all the day long.'"

—James Stark
Bishop, Calvary Apostolic Church, Westerville, Ohio

"If you knew Willie Johnson, it's the reason you're holding this book. If you've never heard of her, it's the reason you should take it home and learn about her life and ministry. In *Through the Waters*, Lori Wagner has done an excellent job painting a picture of a precious, anointed saint of God. When I was growing up, Sister Willie was a member and frequent minister in our church. She was often a guest in our home. Reading the stories in these pages has awakened so many memories.

"Willie Johnson was one of the most powerful ministers in the Pentecostal movement. She touched thousands of lives of men and women all over America with her unique ministry of preaching and song. In a day when there was no social media or videos to record her services, the impact and impression she left on those who were actually there lives on through the memories and testimonies compiled and written in this book. If you would like to be encouraged or challenged to be more faithful and dedicated in your walk with God, add *Through the Waters* to your library.

—Chris Sowards
Pastor, Open Door, Charleston, West Virginia

"Lori Wagner has done an excellent job putting together the life and ministry of Sister Willie Johnson. As I read through the pages of struggle and Apostolic ministry, I was so moved that at times I wanted to weep, and other times to rejoice. Every aspiring minister should have this book as part of his or her library."

—Daniel Garlitz
Bishop, Bonnieview Apostolic Chapel, Keyser, West Virginia

"*Through the Waters* has allowed me to glimpse into the ministerial life of a woman who didn't fit into any mold—and who didn't try to. As a woman whose past included abuse and domestic violence, who is a first-generation Apostolic, an African American, and who has a call to preach and evangelize with a missionary heart, I found myself stirred and challenged by Willie Johnson's refusal to be shaped by our shared realities. Instead of being fashioned by circumstances, she allowed her life and ministry to be molded by the gentle, mending hands of a loving God. Her pain was not in vain. It produced an incredibly impactful ministry to the brokenhearted and bound. Her life in words creates imagery of the Scripture that says, 'The Spirit of the Lord is upon me because He has anointed me to preach.' Open your heart and take the journey through the candid memories and stories that have been laid out in such a captivating way by Lori Wagner they made me wish I could have spoken with Willie Johnson myself. I loved every word."

—Rosalynn Austin
Pastor, One Church, Parkville, Missouri/Kansas City Metro, International Evangelist

"From the opening line, *Through the Waters* immediately captivates the reader. The first song, 'He Washed My Eyes with Tears,' had me wiping tears of my own. As I flipped page after page, I grew continually more intrigued by the life of a woman Jack Cunningham, Billy Cole, James Stark, and Daniel Scott admired, just to name a few.

"Until Lori brought Willie Johnson to life through her written words, I had never heard of this mighty woman of God. I believe every woman in ministry should take the time to read this powerful memoir of a woman sold by her mother, shunned by her father, beaten by her husband, and promoted by God. Your life will be changed forevermore."

—Jessica M. Marquez
Founder and Director, Women Ministering to Women International, Southeast Regional Director, Building the Bridge Ministries

"Lori Wagner did an excellent job of capturing much of Willie Johnson's story. *Through the Waters* is a marvelous tribute to a marvelous evangelist and woman of God."

—Allen Donham
Senior Pastor, Hope Church, Morgantown, West Virginia

AFFIRMING FAITH
8900 Ortonville Road
Clarkston, MI 48348
www.affirmingfaith.org

© 2019 by Lori Wagner

All rights reserved. No portion of this publication may be reproduced, stored in an electronic system, or transmitted in any form or by any means, electronic, mechanical, photocopy, recording, or otherwise, without the prior permission of Affirming Faith. Requests for permission should be addressed in writing to Affirming Faith, 8900 Ortonville Road, Clarkston, MI 48348. Brief quotations may be used in literary reviews.

Scriptures, unless otherwise noted, are taken from the King James Bible, Public Domain.

Printed in the United States of America
Cover and Interior Design: Laura Merchant
Author Photo: Jonathan Main
Edited by: Esther McKinney and Sandra Runkle

Library of Congress Cataloging-in-Publication Data
Names: Wagner, Lori, 1965 – author.
Title: Through the Waters / Lori Wagner
Description: Clarkston : Affirming Faith. | Includes bibliographical references. | Includes index.
Identifiers: LCCN 2018915228 | ISBN 9781733551700 (paperback)
Subjects: LCSH: Christian Women—biography. | African American women—History. | Gifts of the Spirit. | Pentecostals—United States—Biography. | Women in Church Work—History.

DEDICATION

Through the Waters is dedicated
to Daniel and Joretta Scott.

CONTENTS

Appendices

FOREWORD

E vangelist Willie Johnson's life began in a series of conflicts. She was the daughter of a United States senator who crossed racial barriers to father a child he never once acknowledged the entirety of his life. In 1922, her mother, needing money, sold her to an older man to be his 17-year-old bride. Willie's married life became a cruel cross that weighed heavily upon her shoulders, and further emotional anguish culminated with the death of her fourth child, Donald, in 1929. Despite her struggles, when Willie Johnson found a living relationship with God, she became one of the greatest evangelists to ever grace the pulpits of the church.

As Sister Willie's pastor during the late 1950s and throughout the 1960s, my family and I were intimately connected to her life. Outside of the pulpit (and the anointing), it seemed nothing came easy for Willie as she struggled against the debilitating mental strain she worked diligently to overcome. We saw the tears she shed that the rest of the world did not see. We saw her fling herself upon her bed, both physically and mentally exhausted. She leaned heavily upon my words of comfort, and then with a fantastic smile, she would turn to my children with caresses only she could give. My children adored her and considered her "Grandma Willie." While we felt so passionately special in her life, we realized we were not alone. She was a "grandma" to many people. She made everyone feel special in all the churches she visited.

That her story should be told in order to give continuity to her powerful ministry is without question, but how can one weave such a story with tattered threads loosely hanging and little documentation? Those of us who intimately knew Sister Willie Johnson felt completely incapable of accomplishing such a task. It took a professional writer who felt the story should be told—an accomplished researcher who would endeavor to personally contact every living person who had been impacted in any way by Sister Willie's anointed life and ministry. The task required one who would feed the threads into a loom to create the beautiful tapestry this book displays. Lori Wagner has accomplished a nearly impossible mission with excellence.

Lori leads us unerringly through the evident fact that God used Sister Willie's wounds to authenticate a fabulously anointed ministry— one that enabled her to reach into the hearts of thousands of God's suffering constituency and bring healing to those who were hurting. Tender hands placed on tear-stained faces became channels of God's loving care for His own.

Sister Willie ministered in yesterday's America during a time when race was a terribly sensitive subject. Even the church was deeply affected by cultural upheaval, especially in the South, yet Sister Willie ministered in the largest churches from north to south, east and west, and in each, the healing balm continuously flowed.

Readers of *Through the Waters* will be spellbound as chapter after chapter of Sister Willie's ministry of word and song is documented by a myriad of testimonies. This is a story that is long overdue for publishing, and Lori Wagner tells it candidly and truthfully through this work.

—Rev. Daniel Scott
   Pastor, Missionary, Author, Historian
   Adjunct Teacher, Urshan Graduate School of Theology

INTRODUCTION

A sparrow flew through a door into a great banquet hall filled with light, warmth, and food. Moments later, just as quickly as the songbird entered, it flew out another door and vanished into the unknown.

This ancient parable told by a royal advisor to King Edwin of Northumberland in 625 AD, compares the life of a person on earth to a sparrow's swift flight through a room. Willie Johnson was a sparrow in a great hall. A hopeless woman, she once planned to end her life; but on her darkest day, God orchestrated a divine encounter that launched her into full-time ministry. In her new faith walk, the hymn *His Eye is on the Sparrow* became one of Sister Willie's favorite songs. No more would she live discouraged in the shadows. She would sing with joy—happy and free, even as she returned from her glorious experience in the little storefront church to live in the same challenges that had driven her to despair.

The effectiveness of Willie Johnson's ministry cannot be understood apart from her contrasting experiences with harsh adversity and overcoming faith. Raised in West Virginia amid racial segregation, this fatherless, biracial woman rose above her circumstances, social stigma, and cultural limitations by the power of God and fluttered on the church scene with her majestic cape swirling about her shoulders. From the 1930s to the 1980s, God used Sister Willie in revivals of all sizes and varying denominations. Her powerful ministry intermingled song, Scripture, and a unique demonstration of spiritual gifts that were unusual in her day.

As I pieced together fragments of her life, I envisioned Sister Willie fluttering into sanctuaries and lives like the sparrow in the parable. She was a woman of passion—an evangelist who shared God's love and comfort with everyone she met. She knew what it was like to be discouraged and even oppressed, but she also knew the joy of taking flight on the wings of God's love. As she traveled from place to place, she offered her songs of hope, withdrew like a sparrow escaping out a door, and then dashed away to her next assignment. Everywhere she went she touched people, and their lives were forever changed.

I first learned about Willie Johnson decades after she passed. Renowned ministers referenced her in their messages, and her name resurfaced time and again as I researched women in ministry. In 2018, I was compelled to learn more about her. Something in me needed to know Willie Johnson. And now I can say with conviction, she deserves to be honored and remembered.

In this writing, I've attempted to create a mosaic of her life and ministry. She was a woman who seemed larger than life, but Sister Willie was also a real human being. She was dynamic and even breathtaking at times, but she had her share of bloopers, too, along with an incredible warmth that made everyone love her.

Why did Willie Johnson do what she did and at such a great price? How much can we really know about her? What can we learn from her story recreated in this patchwork of testimonies, memories, photos, clippings, and research?

I recently heard a minister say we cannot replicate someone else's ministry, but we can amplify it. Sister Willie had a ministry others might hope to emulate, but it could certainly never be duplicated. I wrote *Through the Waters* with the hope of preserving her legacy and inspiring others to follow in her footsteps, but with the understanding that there was—and ever will be—only one Sister Willie Johnson.

Some through the waters, some through the flood,
Some through the fire, but all through the blood;

Some through great sorrow, but God gives a song,
In the night season and all the day long.

—Lori Wagner

He Washed My Eyes with Tears

Verse 1

He washed my eyes with tears that I might see
The broken heart I had was good for me
He tore it all apart and looked inside
He found it full of fear and foolish pride
He swept away the things that made me blind
And then I saw the clouds were silver lined
And now I understand 'twas best for me
He washed my eyes with tears that I might see

Verse 2

He washed my eyes with tears that I might see
The glory of Himself revealed to me
I did not know that He had wounded hands
I saw the blood He spilt upon the sands
I saw the marks of shame and wept and cried
He was my substitute, for me He died
And now I'm glad He came so tenderly
And washed my eyes with tears that I might see[1]

1   Copyright 1955. Renewed 1983, Ira Stanphill. Assigned New Spring; Catalogs New Spring; Administrators Brentwood-Benson Music Publishing, Inc.

Chapter 1

HE WASHED MY EYES WITH TEARS

The Rescue of Willie Johnson

Bruised and dejected, the tall biracial woman plodded down the street toward the bridge. Enough. She'd just had enough.

The dark river called her to step into the waters and end the misery that was her life.

Just a few more steps and it would all be over.

It was a normal day in Moundsville—at least for everyone else living in the small West Virginia town. Willie meandered her way to her baby's grave. She had to see him one last time before heading to the river. Sorrow engulfed her soul. Hopelessness consumed her. And on top of everything else wrong in her life, it just seemed no one cared.

I don't think I can go on any longer.

Images flashed through Willie's mind as she continued her journey—pictures she had long tried to forget.

Her wedding day. Oh, how she had tried to erase the image that seared into her soul when she witnessed the exchange of money between her husband-to-be, Scott Johnson, and her mother, Louella Cougar. Somehow Louella knew Scott, who was 25 years older than Willie. How they connected was not known, but apparently, when

Louella learned Scott Johnson was looking for a pretty young wife, arrangements were made, and Willie was given to Scott Johnson to have and to hold, if not to love and to cherish.

Willie's parents never married. Her grandmother had been born into slavery, and her mother worked as the housemaid of Daniel Layne, a prominent United States senator from Tennessee. He fathered Willie, but he never acknowledged her as his daughter.

Purchased.

Willie replayed the word that had haunted her for years. She just didn't understand Scott Johnson. She felt not much more than a piece of property to him, but even given her realistic perspective, she could not understand why a man would treat his wife so poorly, especially when he had paid hard-earned money for her.

Willie's fleeting hopes of a good marriage had fallen quickly to the ground with each blow of Scott's thick belt.

Hunger.

Cold.

The gaunt faces of her three children who had so little to eat and no proper clothing.

Each devastating memory propelled Willie forward to the churning river. Life was just not worth living.

Music drifted from an old building across the way and slipped into Willie's revery as she plodded forward in the night. A musically gifted woman, her spirit responded to the melody. The singing was like none she had heard before. It drew her, and she moved toward the sound. As she neared the storefront building on the river road, her thoughts flashed back to an incredible encounter that had taken place after the birth of her first son, Rudolph.

The unexpected meeting began with a dream Willie had that four women were going to come to her and tell her how to "get right" with God. Unknown to her, in Morgantown, approximately ninety miles away, Wilmina Goodin, Ruth Fisher, Goldie Bosley, and Josephine

Poling gathered daily for prayer. The morning after Willie's dream, the Spirit fell in their prayer meeting. One of the women gave a message in tongues, and another interpreted it. Through the gifts of the Spirit, the Lord directed the women to travel to Moundsville to a specific address and ask for a woman named Willie Johnson.

I have chosen her for a great work.

The four women responded immediately and took the train to Moundsville. Once there, they hired a carriage to drive them to the address they were given. It was a hardware store where the women disembarked and inquired with a gentleman inside about a woman named Willie. "That could only be Scott Johnson's wife," said the man, and he told the women how to find the Johnson place out by Parrs Run, a small stream that flowed through Moundsville.

The driver assisted the women into the waiting carriage, climbed onto his perch, and picked up the reins. "Git up," he called to the team. The horses took up the slack in their harnesses, and with a jolt, the carriage lurched forward. Holy expectation filled the women's hearts as they began the final leg of their journey. The carriage took them from the small mining town into the shadows of the forest until the driver was unable to navigate any closer to their destination. He reined in the team near Parrs Run, and the women stepped out onto a woodland path. After a short way, the path broke into a clearing, and nestled in the opening was a home, not much more than a shack. A plume of smoke curled out its chimney, and a woman opened the front door.

Willie Johnson stepped out the door of her home carrying two empty coal buckets. Her dark eyes widened in surprise when she saw the women. She threw the buckets to the ground and cried, "You came! You came! Just like He said you would!"

The four women spent time with Willie and shared the gospel with her. They encouraged her and explained God's salvation plan of repentance, baptism in water in Jesus's name, and the baptism of the Spirit.[2]

---

2   See Acts 2:38.

Following this incredible encounter, Willie's faith surged for a season; but life had remained so very hard and her husband so very mean. She had tried to live out her faith, but darkness eventually choked out the light of hope. In 1925, her second son, Scottie, had been born, and then in 1927, her daughter, Gloria. In 1929, after baby Donald died of acute bronchitis and pneumonia, it seemed to Willie she buried her last bit of hope in the little grave with the tiny body of her lifeless son.

The only way out was the path she now walked to the river.

But that music—that spirited singing coming from the church—it was beautiful.

It won't hurt or change anything if I pause and listen.

Willie stood outside the door for a moment until the singing drew her in. Music had always been a part of her life. As a child, she had sung in the small Baptist church she attended, but this music was different.

Something grabbed ahold of her heart.

When she walked in the door, the scene was unlike anything she was familiar with. People were speaking all at once, their faces lifted to heaven. An evangelist, Bud Entsminger, "preached an old fashioned, tongue-talking, devil-chasing, Apostolic message."[3] Willie was "shaking like Belshazzar" as the minister walked up and down the aisle, preaching about the Holy Ghost.

Her emotions were all over the place, and she chuckled when she saw the fired-up evangelist lift the makeshift Bible stand and carry it from one end of the platform to the other. She'd heard at choir practice, at the Methodist church where she sang, about the Pentecostal preacher who carried the pulpit around when he preached, but she hadn't believed it. Any pulpit she had ever seen was far too heavy to lift with one hand, but this Bible stand was made of orange crates and covered with muslin. Lifting it was not the supernatural feat she had imagined it to be, yet there was something alive and powerful in the service that

---

3   All quotes in Chapter 1 from *Pioneer Pentecostal Women*, vol. 2, compiled by Mary H. Wallace (Hazelwood, MO: Word Aflame Press, 1981).

she could not walk away from, and Willie knew deep in her heart she wanted God—all of God. She responded to the message and received the Holy Ghost. It changed her life, her future, and her eternity.

The joy that filled Willie's heart that night could not be contained. When she left the meeting, she ran out in the street and told everyone who would listen what had happened. She went from person to person and even grabbed the coat of a police officer on the street.

"I just received the Holy Ghost!" she shouted.

The officer pulled away and shook his head. "You received what?"

"I just received the Holy Ghost," she declared with a broad smile and twinkling eyes. "Everybody ought to know what the Holy Ghost is!"

Willie Johnson had just found a reason for living, and live she would—to the fullest and to the glory of God. That night on the way to the river, Willie had planned to end her life, and that is precisely what occurred. Willie's old life had passed away and was replaced with a new, vibrant and Spirit-filled life that would impact others for generations to come.

Little Old Wooden Church Way Out on the Hill

Verse 1

It was in my childhood many years ago
With the Spirit of the Savior
I was filled at an old fashion meeting
My memory lingers still
In that little old wooden church
Way out on the hill

Refrain

You could hear the people singing
About a half a mile away
And your heart begins to get that sudden thrill
It would start your body moving
Till you couldn't keep it still
In that little old wooden church out on the hill

Verse 2

Every Sunday morning
We had our family prayer
Then into that country wagon we would be
Then we'd start out on our journey
Over rocks and over reels
To that little old wooden church way out on the hill

Verse 3

Many folk have passed us
And many folk have gone
But that sweet old golden memory lingers still
I'm gonna keep that Holy Spirit
Till death my body chills
I got it in that wooden church out on that hill[4]

---

4   Words and music by Thomas A. Dorsey, 1949.

Chapter 2

LITTLE OLD WOODEN CHURCH WAY OUT ON THE HILL

The 1930s

Willie Johnson grew up singing songs about God. As a very young girl she sang in a small Baptist church. In later years when she sang *Little Old Wooden Church Way Out on the Hill,* she often envisioned those days in the church of her childhood.[5] In her young adult years, Sister Willie joined a larger Methodist church. She wanted to be a member there so she could sing in their trained choir.[6]

Willie's conversion story spanned several years. The deep call of God began its breakthrough in her life in the mid-1920s when the four women from Morgantown set out to find her. Moundsville, the Johnson's residence at the time, was a small town nestled in the northern panhandle of West Virginia with a population of just over 10,000 people.[7] A ray of light had brightened Willie's darkness, but the oppressiveness of her circumstances continued to reside with her.

---

5   As told in *Pioneer Pentecostal Women.*
6   Per Daniel Scott.
7   Moundsville derived its name from its many Indian burial mounds which include the largest conical burial mound in North America. The town was also home to the West Virginia Penitentiary which operated for over one hundred years. The penitentiary's website claims it to be the site of paranormal activity along with its history of executions and riots. In contrast to these dark realities, Moundsville was also home to the Fostoria Glass Factory where exquisite crystal glassware and lamps were created.

It is believed to have been in 1933, eight or nine years after the four women reached out to her, that Willie received the Holy Ghost in the Entsminger revival and was baptized in Jesus's name by Margaret Barham and Goldie Stewart Basley.[8]

According to 1940 census information, Scott Johnson's highest level of education completed was third grade, and Willie's was fourth grade. Willie was said, however, to have travelled to New York for some formal music training in her teen years. Family friend, Jimmy Ramsey, recalled Willie being trained in opera before she married Scott Johnson and moved to Moundsville. In fact, he recounted Sister Willie in later years mimicking her formal training. Sister Willie told Jimmy she had been taught to sing *hooly, hooly, hooly*, but after she received the Holy Ghost, "She just let her mouth open and sang *holy, holy, holy*."[9]

Scott Johnson worked as a coal miner, and he also did construction and lumber work. During the Depression, he was employed by the Works Progress Administration (WPA), an infrastructure program created in 1935 by President Franklin Roosevelt.[10] The consistency of his work record may reflect entirely on the economy of the day, but the 1940 census depicts him working as a laborer only 32 weeks that year.

In the 1920s and 1930s, the Johnson family lived outside Moundsville by a railroad track where their children were born and raised. Scott didn't like his wife going out much. He did allow her, however, to go into town so she could bring in a bit of money from singing in some of the local churches.[11] Although the 1940 census did not document any income from Sister Willie's singing or ministry, it was said that after she began evangelizing, she became the main breadwinner of the family.[12]

---

8   Details from *Pioneer Pentecostal Women*. James Stark said he knew Margaret Barham who eventually moved to Steubenville, Ohio. He said there were churches in Moundsville and Bridgeport that were outgrowths of that revival brought to the Ohio Valley from someone who had come from Azusa Street.

9   Jimmy Ramsey mentioned this training may have taken place in New York, but he wasn't sure how Sister Willie got there.

10   The WPA ran for eight years during the darkest part of the Great Depression.

11   Per James Stark.

12   Per Daniel Scott and Edwin Harper.

The specifics of how Sister Willie launched into ministry are unknown, and records of her original ministry credentials have not been found. A handwritten note from Sister Willie indicated that she was ordained in 1935 with the Pentecostal Assemblies of Jesus Christ, and documentation is available of her holding license with the organization in 1939 and 1942.

Ministers of the Pentecostal Assemblies of Jesus Christ at a church groundbreaking, early 1930s, Sister Willie second row, fourth from left.

Young Willie Johnson.

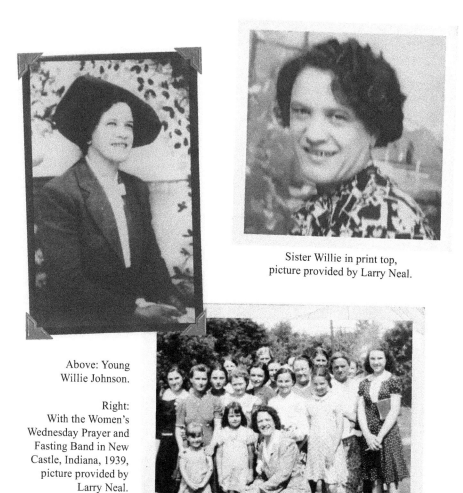

Sister Willie in print top,
picture provided by Larry Neal.

Above: Young
Willie Johnson.

Right:
With the Women's
Wednesday Prayer and
Fasting Band in New
Castle, Indiana, 1939,
picture provided by
Larry Neal.

In 1945, a merger took place between the Pentecostal Assemblies of Jesus Christ and the Pentecostal Church Incorporated. According to her file, it appears Sister Willie transferred her membership to the newly formed United Pentecostal Church International at that time and continued her ministry as a member of the organization for the next 39 years.

In the early days of her ministry, at times, long weeks passed between opportunities to preach. On these occasions, Sister Willie struggled with feelings of abandonment, but she learned to focus on

God and encourage herself despite her emotions. One person recorded her saying, "My Jesus was a lonely Jesus in that garden. So when everybody goes to sleep on you, get on your knees and get deeper, deeper, deeper in God."[13]

Even though she experienced slow seasons, Sister Willie pressed into God, and He continued to enrich and develop her ministry. She was gifted with a unique ability to connect with the Lord and was mightily used in the gifts of the Spirit, especially in words of knowledge that ministered directly to people's needs.

"Sister Willie could go from before *you* to before *God* faster than anyone else I've ever met."

—Chris Sowards

In 1937, with a desperate need in her own life to hear from God, Sister Willie attended the East Central District Conference.[14] Without notice, she was asked to sing, but she was embarrassed because she felt her borrowed dress was too short and too narrow (although it would have been considered modest by most according to the standards of the day). But Sister Willie agreed to sing and filled the meeting with "The Curtain of Time" in such a powerful way she received a personal prophecy about the future success of her ministry.[15]

The Curtain of Time

Verse 1
There's a curtain that's drawn between earth and Heaven
And just beyond lies a beautiful clime
Where the evils of this life no longer can touch me
Lord, let me look past the curtain of time

---

13 Quote from *Pioneer Pentecostal Women*.
14 The East Central District Conference was at the time under the Pentecostal Assemblies of Jesus Christ per Daniel Scott and Edwin Harper.
15 As told by Barbara Davison in *Pioneer Pentecostal Women*.

Refrain

Lord, let me look past the curtain of sorrows and fear
Let me view that sunny bright clime
It would strengthen my faith and would banish all fear
Lord, let me look past the curtain of time

Verse 2

I'm helpless, alone, and I want to see Jesus
And hear the sweet harbor bells chime
Where my friends and dear loved ones are waiting for me
Lord, let me look past the curtain of time

Verse 3

I'm so homesick and blue, and I want to see Jesus
I would like to hear those sweet harbor bells chime
It would brighten my path and would vanish all fear
Lord, let me look past the curtain of time[16]

As Sister Willie ministered to others in their sorrows and needs, she chose to remain in her abusive marriage. She believed that as challenging as her circumstances were, her suffering was the seedbed for the inspiring messages she shared with others.[17]

---

16 Author unknown. Lyrics found in Willie Johnson's songbook printed in Tulsa, Oklahoma, in 1954.
17 Per Daniel Scott.

"HEAR THIS WEEK"

EVANGELIST WILLIE JOHNSON

Nation's Leading Rivalist and Evangelist

Singing and Preaching each Night

At 8 P. M. ━━ *APOSTOLIC CHURCH*

Clark Ave. at West 44th Street

Beginning July 7 through July 21st

Sister Johnson is making her first

appearance in Cleveland

A real thrill awaits you - Cool comfortable seats

Pastor, R. M. HUNGERFORD

Revival in Cleveland, 1930s.

I Trust in God

Verse 1
I trust in God wherever I may be
Upon the land, or on the rolling sea
For come what may, from day to day
My heav'nly Father watches over me

Refrain
I trust in God, I know He cares for me
On mountain bleak or on the stormy sea
Though billows roll, He keeps my soul
My heav'nly Father watches over me

Special
I sing because I'm happy
I sing because I'm free
For His eye is on the sparrow
And I know He watches me[18]

---

18 Words by William C. Martin, 1910; music by Charles H. Gabriel. This special arrangement includes the chorus of "His Eye is on the Sparrow," words by Civilla D. Martin, 1905; music by Charles H. Gabriel.

Chapter 3

I TRUST IN GOD

Family Life During Early Ministry Years

As Willie Johnson's ministry grew wider, deeper, and higher, her domestic situation worsened. Before her marriage, she had known poverty. In fact, in her later years, Sister Willie told her ministerial colleague, Allen Donham, that Scott Johnson gave her mother money on the day of their wedding. Donham noted, "It was an interesting situation. Sister Willie was a singer at the Baptist church and was a very nice young lady, and this guy comes along and says to her mother, 'I'll treat her good, and I want her to be my wife.' The family was not always doing well financially, so Willie's mother accepted Scott Johnson's offer."

Poverty, however, seemed to follow Sister Willie into her married life. The Johnson family experienced financial need in the early years, and their situation became even bleaker during the time of the Great Depression. In his younger days, Scott was said to have been a hardworking man. He had come up with the money to give Willie's mother, after all, but the Johnsons were poor before the Depression hit; and after, Scott never seemed to get back on his feet.[19] Coal miners

---

19 Per David White.

of that time did not make substantial incomes, and there was seldom enough to meet the family's needs.[20]

"She was very poor," said Jimmy Ramsey, who knew the Johnsons after they moved to Charleston in the mid-1940s. "She wasn't making a living at preaching. Back then money was hard to come by." Ramsey spoke of visiting the Johnson home and said, "I've went out there with my brother Eugene to take the children to Sister Willie, but at the same token, I would take her some groceries."

In an interview, Sister Willie reflected on some of the lean years of her ministry. She recalled one time she was preaching at a small, poor church. She stayed with the pastor and there was no food in the house. "Weren't no breakfast," she said, "so we fasted breakfast, knowing God would send dinner. I just said to Him, 'Lord, You who own the cattle on a thousand hills—You just run a little heifer by this way!' And He did. A half beef was delivered in time for our meal."[21]

In the same interview, Sister Willie referenced a time she was ministering in her hometown of Moundsville. "When I went, my stomach's already hungry. I didn't have even a buffalo nickel, but I'm hoping God's gonna bless me with a quarter. Well, they passed the basket, and it wasn't a thing in there, but I ministered like it's been full, 'cause God didn't call me to collect an offering, He called me to preach the Word of God."

Sister Willie left the meeting and went home hungry. When she arrived back at her house, she prayed God would show up with food the same way He had moved so beautifully in the service. While she was praying, someone knocked on the door. "A poor, precious, shabby little sister stood there and told me, 'You know, Sister Willie, I forgot to give you this thirty-five cents I had in my shoe!' And I said, 'Thank You, Jesus! I can get the mush tomorrow and eat for a week!'"[22]

---

20 Per James Stark.
21 Quote from *Pioneer Pentecostal Women.*
22 Ibid.

Sister Willie was so emotional she stuffed her hanky in her mouth to stifle the noises she was making. "If Scott heard . . . I'm gonna sure lose my thirty-five cents and spend this night on the street."[23]

When Sister Willie began evangelizing, she received opposition from her husband. He was against her preaching, and he wanted her home, fixing his meals and ironing his clothes.[24] But Sister Willie would not be dissuaded. She said, "This is my calling, and this is what I have to do. I've got to do this."[25] The family needed the money, so Scott let her go, and then took what she earned when she returned home.[26]

According to Alice Torres, Sister Willie taught herself to drive. "They had an old pickup truck," said Torres, "and she wanted to go preach, so when Scott was passed out from drinking, she took the truck out. She would take the truck keys and tell the kids to come on—they were going preaching. I remember her saying something about the chickens flying out of the way. She and the children would be locked out of the house when they got back."

David White remembered times Sister Willie stayed in the home of his grandfather, W. T. Poling, who pastored Riverside Apostolic in Morgantown, West Virginia. When she was in the Poling's home, Scott would call her. White said Sister Willie tried to hide the majority of the conversation between them, but it was the era before cordless phones, and it was clear the conversation was terse.

White also remembered a specific time Scott Johnson showed up at his grandfather's house to fetch Sister Willie home. Brother Poling, a 6'7"-tall man, went out to deal with him. He brought Scott in the house and spent quite a bit of time with him in his office. Scott left the Poling home without incident.

---

23 Ibid.
24 Per David White.
25 Ibid.
26 Per Edwin Harper and Alice Torres.

Scott Johnson manipulated his wife. He was said to have threatened to kill himself to keep Willie in line.[27] On one occasion he forced Sister Willie to go to the telephone company and ask them to move a pole that stood in front of the Johnson house. When the telephone company denied the request, Scott admitted that he had known all along they wouldn't do it. The business had the right of way. He just wanted to see if his wife would do what he said.[28]

Scott either did not have the money to buy coal or simply refused to buy it. Everyone in the valley heated with coal then, and the coal trains would come through the mine camps. Coal fell off the trains when they started and stopped, and Scott would send his wife and children out to gather coal in their baskets. That's how they heated their house.[29] In fact, people who worked on the railroad would throw coal off the train into the Johnson's yard so Sister Willie would have heat and be able to use the cookstove she made on a car engine hood.[30]

When Sister Willie was first licensed and ministering in the East Central District of the Pentecostal Assemblies of Jesus Christ, she had only two dresses. She washed one dress and wore the other every night until Brother Frank Curts, a leader in the District, took note, and made arrangements for his wife to get Sister Willie a second dress.[31]

Scott berated Sister Willie and seemed to relish his power over her.[32] Many people knew of Scott's domineering verbal mistreatment, but not everyone was aware of the extent of the abuse Sister Willie endured. Several people reported that Scott Johnson was an alcoholic.[33]

---

27   Per David White.
28   Per Daniel Scott.
29   James Stark lived with his grandparents until the fifth grade, and Sister Willie stayed in their house when he was a boy. He heard her tell stories at the dinner table and when sitting around visiting after church.
30   Per Kenneth Mendenhall, Daniel Scott, and Alice Torres.
31   Per Larry Neal.
32   Per Daniel Scott, Michell Cole, and Linda McGinnis.
33   Per Chris Sowards, Stephen Long, and Alice Torres.

He was said to be "uncaring" and "stern,"[34] and several recalled his "mean" and "rough" treatment.[35] One person who knew Sister Willie during the time her husband was alive said it was "very sad the way he treated her."[36] Another said Scott locked his wife in her room two weeks at a time and destroyed her things.[37]

The amount or severity of any physical abuse inflicted on Sister Willie would be hard to document, but Sister Willie confided in people close to her that Scott beat her.[38] One person heard her speak of him beating her with a miner's belt. This would not have been a regular "hold-your-pants-up" belt; it was a tool belt up to three or four inches wide.[39] Another person quoted Sister Willie's own words, "He gave me a spanking. He gave me a whipping."[40] But aside from the hardship, Sister Willie said, "I had made a vow, and I wasn't going to forsake that vow."[41] Chris Sowards, current pastor of Open Door Church in Charleston, West Virginia, heard Sister Willie tell his parents about a time she was so discouraged the Lord asked her if she wanted Him to kill Scott for her. "She said it scared her," said Sowards, "and she said, 'No.'"

If Sister Willie wasn't home by a certain time at night, most often after a church service, Scott locked the door, now and again throwing her few clothes out on the street as well.[42] Sometimes she would sleep in the coal bin which was a covered lean-to attached to the back of the house. Other times, she just slept at the front of the house on the glider on the porch and comforted herself by singing, "My Heavenly Father watches over me."[43]

---

34 Per Bob Gilstrap and Frank Glasco
35 Per George Adams, Jimmy Ramsey, David White, Bob Gilstrap, Donald Haymon, and Allen Donham.
36 Per Bob Gilstrap.
37 Per Chris Sowards.
38 Per Jimmy Ramsey.
39 Per James Stark.
40 Per Edwin Harper and Alice Torres.
41 Per Edwin Harper.
42 As recorded in *Pioneer Pentecostal Women.*
43 As recorded in *Pioneer Pentecostal Women*; glider mentioned by Daniel Scott; lyrics from the song "I Trust in God" by William C. Martin.

When Scott Johnson awakened in the mornings, he would unlock the door and let her in to cook his breakfast.[44] Later in life, Sister Johnson reflected on those nights she slept outside and said, "You know, the foxes have their holes, the birds of the air have their nests, but Jesus didn' have nowhere to lay down His head. Now here, I had that doorstep! My Heavenly Father watches over me."[45]

> "I have heard of her coming home after a mighty move of God and her husband waiting for her on the porch in the dark. I heard that he swung and hit her halfway up the steps busting her mouth and nose, rolling her back down the steps and hill into the yard. He just left her lying there. He went in the house and locked the door. She slept on the porch again that night. . . . She had a very heavy cross to bear."
>
> —Randy Witt

Sister Willie also spoke of Scott's cruelty to their children, but it is unknown if he was physically abusive to them.[46] There were times he locked his wife out but he did allow the children to go inside.[47] More than one person recounted how Scott tied the salt and pepper shakers to a string and nailed them to his side of the table because he didn't want the children to touch them.[48]

The accounts of Sister Willie's home life may seem unbelievable, but people who lived outside the Moundsville community bore witness to them. Marie McElhaney once traveled from Indiana to Sister Willie's home. Larry Neal, a member of the McElhaney's church, shared Marie's report, "She came back and told our church, and she said everything Sister Willie said about her living conditions was true. Scott Johnson was a controller."

---

44   Per James Stark, LaVona Sauters, Jimmy Ramsey, and Edwin Harper.
45   Quote from *Pioneer Pentecostal Women.*
46   Per James Stark.
47   Per Daniel Scott.
48   Per Alice Torres.

At times, Sister Willie gave money to her neighbors to take care of the children for her when she traveled, but that wasn't always enough.[49] Scott was known to have used his children to manipulate his wife. When Sister Willie was away, he at times locked the children out of the house so they would go to the company store in the mining camp to use the phone, track Sister Willie down, and tell her she needed to come home.[50]

Through all of this, Sister Willie subjected herself to her husband.[51] She could be in the middle of a revival, but when Scott told her to come home, she would close down the meeting and go back to Moundsville to attend to whatever it was he wanted done. Then he would let her go back out again so she could make more money.[52] This situation made evangelizing a great challenge.[53]

"When he [Scott Johnson] was ready for her to come home, he would call and say, 'Shut it down!'"

—Vesta Mangun

"She could be in the middle of an amazing revival, and if he called and said come home, she would go."

—Chris Sowards

"She was married to a man who was not saved, and he gave her strict orders as to when she could go and preach and when she couldn't. Whenever she got news from him that she was to come home, she went home, regardless of the revival. She was very obedient to him."

—Jack Leaman

---

49 Per Douglas Rashall.
50 Per James Stark and *Pioneer Pentecostal Women*.
51 Per Daniel Scott.
52 Per James Stark and Bob Gilstrap.
53 Per Bob Gilstrap.

"My dad, Paul Lawrence, was a carpenter and did small jobs for Sister Willie, so we were at her home several times.[54] My mother told me what little she knew about Sister Johnson's life; that she had an abusive husband. How often she knew that when she got home from church she was in for trouble, yet this was not a deterrent. She considered it a privilege to suffer for the name of Jesus.

"Tears rolled down her face when she gave her testimony and encouraged saints to stay faithful to the Lord even during hard times and that God would strengthen and sustain them through anything they might face. I remember feeling like I wanted to be a real lady of God when I heard her testimony. I wanted to be someone that was not 'put on,' but deep-down real with God."

—Debby Harrah

Scott's oppression of Sister Willie's faith included refusing to allow her to pray aloud in her own home.[55] It was said, however, that in his later years he softened a good bit;[56] and before he passed away, he asked his wife to pray for him.[57] For all the grief and suffering Willie Johnson endured in her home, she was heard by more than one person saying her life and ministry would not be what they were if not for her relationship with her husband.

"If there hadn't been a Scott, there would never have been a Willie."[58]

—Willie Johnson

---

54 Paul Lawrence received the infilling of the Holy Ghost in one of Sister Willie's tent revivals in Kanawha City, West Virginia.
55 Recorded in *Pioneer Pentecostal Women*.
56 Per James Stark.
57 Recorded in *Pioneer Pentecostal Women*.
58 Per James Stark.

No one person knew all the resistance and difficulties Sister Willie faced, but when she ministered to others, she did communicate the general idea of her husband's opposition and resistance. She made it evident in her sermons that she faced challenges in her home. She spoke about her husband who wasn't living for God and how he was "doing this" and "doing that" and "wouldn't let me do that."[59]

> "I believe her past life was so horrible she found a life in God she would never have known any other way. She knew after she had been out having great revival services her husband was going to beat her and lock her out on the front porch. That took some true spunk."
>
> —Linda McGinnis

> "Sister Willie Johnson preached and prophesied . . . even though it meant that she would be beaten by her husband for doing so or made to stay outside on the porch . . . she still preached under an anointing so strong that when she walked down the aisle, people felt the power of God."
>
> —Deborah Simmons-Garcia

During the early 1950s, Sister Willie often preached revivals for young Pastor Wayne Trout in Wilmington, Delaware. She and her evangelistic companion, Charlene Day, often stayed in his home two weeks at a time. During one of those revivals, Howard Goss[60] was also visiting the Trouts. Driving from his home in Canada, the Trout's home was a convenient stop-over as Goss traveled across the United States to various churches. He did this often.

"One night after service," said Trout, "we were sitting in the living room. The phone rang; it was Sister Willie's daughter telling her that her dad was yelling and screaming and was demanding she come home

---

59 Per Bob Gilstrap.
60 Howard Goss was the first General Superintendent of the United Pentecostal Church International.

immediately. When Sister Willie hung up the phone, she was crying and stated, 'I have endured this so many years, and I don't know how much more I can put up with it. Every time I go to preach a revival, he calls and demands me to come home.'

"At that point, Brother Goss laid his big hands on Sister Willie and said, 'Gather 'round. We are going to pray.' After our prayer meeting, the spirit of heaviness lifted. Brother Goss told her that the Lord would not put more on her than she could bear.

"A half-hour later, the phone rang. It was her daughter Gloria again, and she told Sister Willie her husband had just passed away. 'Stay and finish the revival!' said Gloria. Sister Willie stayed one more night, and on that night, six or eight received the Holy Ghost. The next day, she returned to West Virginia."

Until Scott Johnson's death in 1957, he resisted his wife's ministry, attempted to keep her from it, and even shut it down at times; but because he benefited from the money it brought in, he allowed her to go. Of her suffering, Sister Willie said in an interview, "Upon some of His children He's put a special cross, because He can trust that child to bear it, and grow in Him. Suffering is a ministry in itself."

She went on to say, "He loves us so much, now, that He knows when we get to the crisis place (and He also leads His ministers to the crisis place to help them so they can help you), first, you gotta go there yourself, before you can help anybody. He takes me to the backside of the desert, then I know how you feel. . . . And that's why He took upon Himself flesh." The interviewer noted Sister Willie paused and smiled "that soft Willie smile" and then said, "God truly ministers in brokenness." True to her form, she followed her incredible insights with the words of a song, "I trust in God, I know He cares for me."[61]

When asked how Sister Willie coped with the dysfunction and abuse in her home while simultaneously ministering to others, her

---

61 As recorded in *Pioneer Pentecostal Women.*

former pastor, Daniel Scott, said, "She didn't connect the two. When she walked out of that home it was into a different world."

That "different world" included regular visits to the Moundsville prison. Larry Neal remembered Sister Willie telling him of her times ministering to the inmates. "She preached in the Moundsville prison," said Neal, "and she sang and walked up and down between the cells. She said the men would weep and put their hands through the bars and try to touch her as she was singing, 'The Love of God.'"

Consecrated

Consecrated, Lord, I want to be
So I might be better with Thee
For I know if my mind is stayed on Thee
You said you would keep my mind in perfect peace
Consecrate my heart, dear Lord, today
Consecrate my mind right now, Oh, Lord, I pray
And help me to live each day for Thee
Oh, I know, I know I am thine[62]

---

62 Author unknown.

Chapter 4

CONSECRATED

Living for God

For those who experienced the ministry of Sister Willie Johnson, to remember her was to remember her cape. Throughout most of her years of ministry, she wore a "preaching uniform" that included a sleeveless cloak.[63] People who did not have the opportunity to be in her presence and experience her humble spirit might assume her cape was showy. Yes, Sister Willie "worked" her cape. She was dramatic because she was passionate, but not one person accused her of being showy in a garish, pompous way.

Sister Willie in her preaching uniform.

---

63 Sister Willie had more than one cape. It was often solid white with a black bead around the edge, and there were some that were black satin on the outside and white on the inside, per Daniel Scott.

Her cape was considered by some to show her respect for the pulpit. She would not step behind the sacred desk to minister without it.[64] When she evangelized, her ensemble resembled a nurse's uniform—a white dress, a cape, white stockings, and simple shoes. She looked the part of a servant.[65]

> "She always wore a white, long-sleeved, buttoned-up dress[66] and a large cape, and when she would get anointed in the Spirit and walk about preaching and singing, that cape would swirl around!"
>
> —Debby Harrah

Sister Willie did not wear her preaching uniform every day or to every service she attended. One congregant, LaVona Sauters, recalled a time she saw a well-dressed woman sitting in the front section of her church in a service at Christ Temple. She did not recognize the woman from behind, but it turned out to be Sister Willie. She was asked to the platform to minister, but she would not go to the pulpit without her uniform. She did, however, sing a song from the piano.

Ministering in an era when preaching was done predominantly by men, Sister Willie took care to be well covered. Several people confirmed that she wore her cape for modesty's sake. She was a beautiful woman, and she did not want her figure or appearance to be a stumbling block.[67] When asked by Lois Truman why she wore it, Sister Willie confided to her that she perspired profusely when she preached and she did not want to be distracted by wondering about her appearance.[68] Sister Willie always dressed carefully and looked very nice.[69]

---

64 Per LaVona Sauters.

65 Ibid.

66 Larry Neal recalled it was by the '50s Sister Willie began to wear all-white when she ministered.

67 As noted in *Pioneer Pentecostal Women* and by Alice Torres.

68 Larry Neal said, "She needed the cape. By the time she finished preaching, she was wet from perspiration."

69 Per LaVona Sauters.

Sister Willie's cape was a component of her unique storytelling, song-singing, hope-inspiring ministry. She would flip her cape back when she was emphasizing a point.[70] One moment she would be on one side of a church singing, "Oh, how I love Him." As she lifted the words, she swang out an arm and her cape would flare. Then, with arm extended, she would walk to the other side of the room singing, "How I adore Him" and then throw out her other arm.[71] Randy Witt said, "I can still hear her voice and see that cape swinging like the wings of an angel."

"As children, we respected her and had the 'fear' of the power that was manifest in her ministry. When I was six or seven years old, a few of us were talking about her beautiful satin cape. We were arguing if it was magic or not and what would happen if we touched it.

"Since we were allowed to sit on the front bench if we behaved, one day we decided we would touch it when she walked by. But then we thought something terrible would happen if we did—the power of God might strike us dead— so we chickened out. One girl who didn't always come to church was brave enough to quickly touch it as Sister Willie passed by. Since God has mercy on silly little girls, nothing happened, but we sure respected our friend's bravery. Sister Willie would have laughed about that."

—Neva Limones

"My mom made her big, long, white dresses for her and her black capes lined with silk," said Chris Sowards. "Her dresses were like choir robes, and when she would spin and move around, the cape spun with her." Sowards called Sister Willie "an intimidating figure."

---

70   Per Neva Limones.
71   Per LaVona Sauters.

BLOOPERS

Sister Willie's uniforms had buttons running vertically down the center of the top to the waistband. One night as she was ministering, she threw her cape to the side, and when she did, all the buttons popped open all the way down. Daniel Scott vividly remembered their eye contact and his signal to her that her top was open. "She didn't stop ministering," he said. "She wrapped her cape around her and started being 'shut in with God,' and when she came out from that drape, she was buttoned up."

Chris Sowards told of a day Sister Willie's slip fell off while she was preaching. "'Everybody raise your hands and praise the Lord,' she said. And while they did, she pulled her slip up and went right on preaching."

Linda McGinnis also remembered a time Sister Willie lost her slip while preaching. "She asked everyone to close their eyes, and she kicked it under the pulpit and picked it up later. No one knew the difference."

"She was always in a hurry. She always wore the cape and then would put on a sweater. One night we were running late and she grabbed her sweater and cape and rolled them up. When we got to the church, she was coming in the back speaking to people. The music had started and it was time to go up. A man saw her drop something. It was her girdle. She had accidentally rolled it in with her sweater and cape and it had fallen out from under her sweater and onto the floor.

"The man said, 'Sister Willie! Sister Willie! I believe you dropped something.'

"She looked down at her girdle on the floor of the church and hollered, 'Oh, Jesus!' Then she scooped it up and took off to the platform. Those were normal things for her."

—David White

Beyond Sister Willie's distinctive physical appearance, her personality and presence were unforgettable, as well. When Willie Johnson entered a room, people felt the presence of God in her and moving through her.[72] Over and again the word "powerful" was used to describe her ministry.

> "She had a very, very strong presence. She was bigger than life. Gregarious. She walked into a room, and she made a grand entrance. She was in command—not in a funny way, but very loving, very kind. I remember her hands as being strong and soft. I remember her picking me up when I was a little boy and holding me, rocking me."
>
> —James Stark

> "She was a humble person—not into 'self'—but she really came on strong when she got under the anointing."
>
> —David Fauss

> "Back in those days a lot of times people traveled in teams—women did. I remember I had Sister Willie and Charlotte the converted nun at my house at the same time. Charlotte never came out of her room, but Willie was—oh man—she was high energy and having a good time. Her personality was godly, jovial, and she had gravitas."
>
> —Kenneth Mendenhall

Sister Johnson, for all her vivacious energy and persona, carried with her a seriousness—an importance of what she was doing that caused others to respect and trust her. She truly loved God and she truly loved people. She always had a sweet disposition.[73]

---

72 Per LaVona Sauters.
73 As told to Cynthia Roy by her mother, Goldie Goddard.

"She was a very outgoing, loving person who in my opinion really had a deep, genuine love for people. Even though she went through all kinds of hurt and pain, it didn't make her bitter. It didn't make her angry. She wanted to make the lives of people she came in contact with—she wanted to leave them better than she met them and to help them know just a little of the grace, mercy, and love of Jesus Christ. She was very, very kind."

—Roger Zimmerman

"Everybody loved her. She was so jovial. We had people who came to our church, and they only came once a year when she was there holding a revival. My dad called them *Willieites*."[74]

—Jimmy Ramsey

"She never met a person she didn't know. There was no stranger. It didn't matter who you were, she would go right up and talk to you. It didn't make any difference if she was on the street or in the church. She was very outgoing and vivacious. She just automatically drew people to her because of her personality. She was fun."

—David White[75]

David White remembered Sister Willie going to town with his mother and grandmother. Sister Willie would hold conversations with people in the store. She would talk to a clerk for twenty minutes while people were trying to check out.

"She was just gabbing," he said, "she just kept on, kept on, kept on. She was the type of person that if she was in town and she went by someone and she thought they needed prayer, she stopped and

---

74 Jimmy Ramsey's father, Dewey Ramsey, served as assistant pastor of Open Door Church in Charleston, West Virginia, in 1945.
75 Grandson of W. T. Poling who pastored Riverside Apostolic in Morgantown and also served as the second West Virginia District Superintendent for the United Pentecostal Church International.

would go to them and say, 'Listen, I just feel you are in need of prayer,' and she would pray with them right on the street. It was just part of what she was."

"It's hard to describe someone's personality when you mainly knew them from the pulpit, but I would think she was probably a very kind individual. She was extremely Holy Ghost-filled. Her messages were . . . you just knew they were from the Lord."

—George Adams

Randy Witt said Sister Willie had an "infectious kindness" and remembered her "calling most everyone younger than her 'child' as she ministered to them." Witt said, "She was so kind and loving. She was *real!*"

"To me, she was affectionate. Always willing to greet you. She would shake your hand and hold on to you with both hands to look you in the eye.

"I always felt like she was 'reading my mail!' And there is no doubt that she could do that! Whenever she was coming to preach at the church; I would always repent again just to be sure there was no dirty laundry lying out so to speak!"

—Randy Witt

"When it was announced she was coming to town, everybody knuckled down and prayed up before she got there."

—Roger Zimmerman

"If you announced she was coming and gave a date, people started fasting and praying to get their lives right before she got there. That's a fact."

—Edwin Harper

"Her personality was warm and friendly. She could laugh and have fun. When she laughed, she laughed all over. Her whole physical body was laughing. She shook when she laughed. She would throw her head back and laugh greatly.

"I haven't pastored Sister Willie for over fifty years, but she's been an awesome figure in my life. I remember once when my wife and children and I drove to Dallas and we didn't tell her we were coming. When we walked into the church, she hollered, 'Charleston!'"

—Daniel Scott[76]

"Her personality (I think) was molded by God. The things she went through molded her and made her very compassionate. She knew what she had gone through, and yet she was able *not* to withdraw, but to be a broken vessel. She could truly just be herself with you—with the audience—and the Holy Ghost would truly use her for the glory of God.

"She was quite a character, and I say that in the most respectful way. When I pastored, she would sometimes be preaching to us in the church, have a shouting time, then holler out the window, 'Hey, you out there, you can have this, too.' Everyone in the area, inside the church and outside, knew Sister Willie was preaching."

—Allen Donham

"She was a no-nonsense person, but she wasn't standoffish or anything like that. She was very approachable and very gracious. She took what she did very seriously. She did pray and seek the mind of God, and she was totally devoted to the ministry."

—Lois Truman

---

76 Daniel Scott pastored Sister Willie in Charleston at Open Door Apostolic Church from 1959–1969.

Sister Willie had what some people called the "Willie look."

"She had certain ways to look when making a point. Looking
through eyelashes with her head held at an angle. Eyes rolling
upward when something was humorously unbelievable, or
down her nose to illustrate someone's superior attitude. The
'faces' were always in humor and good taste to illicit mirth
from the hearers. She held the congregations spellbound. I
am telling you, she was a master in the pulpit."

—Daniel Scott

"Sister Willie was a woman who liked to laugh. It just
seemed she was always smiling. The joy of the Lord was
on her face always. She was kind and gentle. She never
promoted herself, and I never knew her to show anger or any
mean spirit. You felt that she cared about you."

—Neva Limones

"She really helped my mom through so much with my father!
My mom, Eva Underwood, loved her so much! Sister Willie
always called to make sure she was alright!"

—Teresa Underwood

"We weren't important people. My dad was a backslider
and my mom the pianist. We weren't anyone special, but she
knew us personally. She called me by my name. She wasn't
afraid to be friends with people."

—LaVona Sauters

"There was a real funny side to her. She was very serious in
service, but we had so much fun in the home. She was a hoot.
She would laugh and we would kid and totally relax and have
a big time like you would have with your family. She was
very warm and compatible.

"Sister Willie was in touch with God and had such a walk with God, but yet she could be so human. She was close to people. She had groupies—people who followed her around in Oklahoma if they could drive. That's why we'd have such a crowd. People from Tulsa and other towns would come. She would become acquainted with them, and she didn't become isolationist. She gave herself readily to friends and friendships.

"Many times in her sermons she would talk about her *honchy*. I had never heard the word. There was a lady in her home church that was her trial—she was a nuisance. I don't remember what all she would do, but she would get in her face and in her life and say things and do things to tantalize her. Maybe she didn't do it purposely. She may have been ignorant and didn't know how to treat people, but Sister Willie called her *honchy*. I don't know the legitimacy of that word, but even after she would leave, someone would refer to someone else and call them a *honchy*. It became a word in our family, even with our church people who would refer to their *honchy* (like a thorn in the flesh)."

—Bob Gilstrap[77]

"I quote Sister Willie, 'When everyone would testify, Sister South would heartily say, 'Oh, yes, Lord, Amen. Bless her, Lord!' But when I'd testify, she'd groan, 'Oh, me. Help us, Jesus!'[78] She was my sandpaper to grind me and polish me for Him. You've got to have 'sandpaper people' in your life, saints!"

—Larry Neal

"She was dynamic. I never really met anybody like her. I was a young boy—maybe eleven or twelve when I received

---

77 Bob Gilstrap knew Sister Willie from many revivals she held in Oklahoma.
78 Larry Neal said, "Sister South was a lady in Sister Willie's home church when she was a young saint."

the Holy Ghost. She was captivating. Even as a kid, I loved to hear her preach and sing, and the presence of the Lord was just so strong. Very few women had that kind of affect in the ministry, and she was one of them that I just respected so much."

—William Finn

God Leads Us Along

Verse 1

In shady, green pastures, so rich and so sweet
God leads His dear children along
Where the water's cool flow bathes the weary one's feet
God leads His dear children along

Refrain

Some through the waters, some through the flood
Some through the fire, but all through the blood
Some through great sorrow, but God gives a song
In the night season and all the day long

Verse 2

Sometimes on the mount where the sun shines so bright
God leads His dear children along
Sometimes in the valley, in darkest of night
God leads His dear children along

Verse 3

Though sorrows befall us and evils oppose
God leads His dear children along
Through grace we can conquer, defeat all our foes
God leads His dear children along

Verse 4

Away from the mire, and away from the clay
God leads His dear children along
Away up in glory, eternity's day
God leads His dear children along[79]

---

79 Words and music by George A. Young, 1903.

Chapter 5

GOD LEADS US ALONG

The 1940s

Goldie Entsminger was a very close friend to Sister Willie; and her husband, Bud, had a great impact on Sister Willie's ministry.[80] Not only did Bud Entsminger preach the revival that turned her life around, when he later founded the Open Door Mission in Charleston, West Virginia, Sister Willie called this ministry her spiritual home. In the mid-1940s, the Johnson family relocated from Moundsville to Sissonville, a small community north of Charleston, West Virginia, in an area known as Slip Hill. According to family friend, Jimmy Ramsey, the move took place in 1946 or 1947 and happened because Sister Willie wanted to be closer to Open Door.

After the move, Scott took a job at Mountain State Hospital.[81] "I visited Scott at the hospital," said Ramsey, "but I couldn't get him to come

---

80 Per Daniel Scott. Bud Entsminger was a man of compassion and influence. He was a signer of the charter for the Tri-State Council of Apostolic Ministers. In 1945, he was at the meeting at Whiteway Tabernacle in St. Louis, Missouri, and a voting member when the Pentecostal Assemblies of Jesus Christ and the Pentecostal Churches Incorporated merged to become the United Pentecostal Church International. He was esteemed by his fellow ministers as well, and pictures from annual General Conference meetings place him as sitting among the officials.
81 The hospital featured 120 beds, two operating rooms, a delivery room and nursing school. Mountain State merged with Charleston Memorial Hospital in 1969 and closed in 1971.

to church. I talked to him about Sister Willie and how powerful she was. He'd say, 'I know she's got something, but I don't know what it is.'"[82]

Sister Willie and B. G. Entsminger.

Open Door Mission, 1937, Founder B. G. Entsminger pictured at far right wearing a suit.

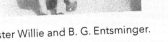

Revival at Open Door Church, *Charleston Gazette,* 1949.

OLD TIME APO'   C REVIVAL
BEGIN

SUNDAY NIGHT, AUG.   0 P. M.
CONTINUING UNTIL   18

The location is at the end of Reyn.   St. back of Dr.
Duke's Hospital, entrance off Va. St. Evangelist Willie
Johnson is an outstanding evangelist of the Apostolic faith.
Sister Johnson's God-inspired sermons and songs are a
blessing to all.

Come! Don't miss this wonderful refreshing from Heaven.
This tent meeting is under the auspices of th. Open Door
Apostolic Mission, 205 Brown St., Charleston, W. Va. Rev.
B. G. Entsminger extends a welcome to all.

Also remember to tune in WGKV 1490 on your dial every
Sunday morning 7 to 7:30 and listen to The Open Door
Apostolic Mission Young People, in song and Rev. B. G.
Entsminger, pastor, bringing forth the Word of God.

---

82 Jimmy Ramsey believed the Johnsons moved to Charleston in 1946 or 1947 because of the timeline of Entsminger's ministry. He said the work on Virginia Street opened in 1937; Open Door Mission opened in the 1940s; and the church on Brown Street was built around 1943 or 1944. Ramsey said the ministry was not known as Open Door Apostolic Church until around 1944 when the church on Brown Street was dedicated.

Before his conversion, Bud Entsminger had been a prize fighter. When he came to faith in God, he left that profession and joined the Volunteers of America where he reached the rank of captain. After receiving the Holy Ghost and a revelation of the oneness of God, he founded Open Door Mission in Charleston, an Apostolic compassion ministry that provided food, clothing, and shelter to the needy. He had a burden to reach the poor and hurting with the love of God, the saving power of the gospel, and to provide practical help for physical needs.[83] Later in his ministry, Entsminger also opened a home to provide medical care to the poor elderly.

The Entsmingers's work became well known throughout West Virginia, and after Bud affiliated with the United Pentecostal Church, it became known as the Open Door Apostolic Mission.

Bud Entsminger had a radio program that broadcast on WKNA radio station. Every time he signed off he would say, "This is Bud Entsminger, your converted prize fighter." Early in the 1950s, Entsminger developed throat cancer. It was advanced. A tumor had grown in his throat, and Entsminger asked Sister Willie to pray for him.

"I won't pray for you, Cap," answered Sister Willie, "You leave the program with everyone thinking you're a prize fighter. You *were* a prize fighter, and Jesus saved you from that."

After Entsminger promised to never again use the phrase, Sister Willie agreed to pray for him. She picked up a bottle of olive oil and said, "Bud, open your mouth." The minister complied, and Sister Willie poured about a half a bottle of oil down his throat in the name of Jesus. God instantly healed him of cancer. He lived several more years.[84]

In 1941, Albert E. Kelbaugh (at the age of around 25) was diagnosed with tuberculosis. In order to protect his family from infection, he admitted himself to Hopemont Sanitarium where he expected to die.

---

83 www.wvgazettemail.com/news/moments-in-time-the-open-door-mission/article_
be65abda-06de-51ec-a12d-4f0f27214c88.html.
84 Per Daniel Scott.

Albert knew nothing about the Scriptures, but after three months in the sanitarium, he decided to read the Gideon Bible in his room. He read the book of Genesis, and the words caused him to reflect on God and His power. "If God created man," Kelbaugh said to himself, "He can repair him."

Kelbaugh was so ill he couldn't speak. His larynx had deteriorated, one lung was two-thirds gone, and the other was one-third gone. A few days after reading the Bible, Kelbaugh packed a small cardboard suitcase, dropped it out the window and climbed out after it. He thumbed a ride to the train station, jumped a freight train, and traveled home to greet his wife who was greatly surprised to see her sick husband.

For two weeks after his return, Kelbaugh and his wife sat outside in the cool of the evenings. Each night, they heard singing in the distance, and on a Friday they decided to attend the revival meeting being held by John Carr, the local Apostolic pastor, at the gospel tent. The evangelist was Willie Johnson.

The people were "having a time." And the crowd was so thick the Kelbaughs found no place to sit, so they stood in the back and then walked home. Saturday they went to a second meeting. During the service, Sister Willie invited everyone who needed something from God to come to the front, and both husband and wife went forward and turned their lives over to God. The next day the couple was baptized in the Ohio River in Jesus's name, and with great expectation, they returned to the tent for evening service where both husband and wife again responded to the altar call.

Albert Kelbaugh was so weak he could not raise his arms. No sound came from his mouth when he tried to speak, but as he began praying, he burst out in a loud voice speaking in tongues. His wife saw what had happened to him, and she, too, received the Holy Ghost.

The next day, Kelbaugh had a unique encounter with God. He was outside for four hours, and a crowd eventually gathered around him. The people thought he had lost his mind. Someone went to find Sister Willie and tell her about it. After she arrived, Kelbaugh came to himself and claimed his healing. Immediately, he began to gain weight and strength, and soon, after three and a half years of being unable to work, Albert Kelbaugh returned to his job. He had received a miracle, and his doctor verified his lungs were clear of tuberculosis.[85]

In the early 1940s Sister Willie ministered at Kanawha City Holiness Church for Pastor O. J. Smalley. This was one of the pioneer Pentecostal churches in the area.[86] She ministered in Bedford, Indiana, and San Jose, California, as remembered by Jody Hussein. "I remember the first time I saw her," said Hussein. "I was a small child who had trouble sitting still. I remember her fire and preaching. I was afraid to move a muscle. When she came off the platform swiftly, I ducked for cover, because I knew I had been naughty."

"Sister Willie was from my home church in Charleston, West Virginia, Open Door Apostolic. She would make you freeze and quiver at the same time, and if she came in your direction . . . *Oh, no! She knows!*"

—Dave Ramsey

Delores Ramsey recalled the unique circumstances under which she came to know Sister Willie:

"I was thirteen in 1944. My mom was never Pentecostal. She would cuss worse than a sailor. I remember her smoking a pipe, but she loved Sister Willie, and that's how I started going to Open Door. My mom heard Sister Willie was holding a revival there."

---

85   This is a retelling of the account recorded by Doug Joseph in *The Life and Ministry of Billy and Shirley Cole* (Booksurge Publishing: Nitro, 2007), 3–9. Albert E. Kelbaugh was the father of Shirley Cole.
86   Per Jimmy Ramsey.

Sister Willie's daughter, Gloria (2nd from left), with Kathleen Cooper and family.

From 1945–47, Delores, then known by her maiden name Holsteen, sang in a trio with Kathleen Cooper and Mary Whitten. "We would go to a little church in Henderson with Sister Willie," said Delores. "It was a home mission church, and we went for the revivals. Kathleen would play accordion for the group and for Sister Willie."

Sister Willie held revivals in Charleston at least two or three times a year, and at least once a year at Open Door. "I had a close friendship with her," said Delores.

"I remember going out to eat with her many times," added Teresa Schanzer, Delores's daughter, "and my father worked many times on her old Cadillac."

In April, 1949, Sister Willie preached a revival at Riverside Apostolic Church in Morgantown, West Virginia. Fifty-eight people received the Holy Ghost.[87] Her ministry touched the lives of men and women there who were themselves propelled into full-time ministry.

In one revival service, Sister Willie prayed with a young teen, Jack Yonts, and he received the Holy Ghost.[88] Yonts became a minister, and his life had a far-reaching impact, including the establishment of the Christmas for Christ program to support the work of home missionaries in December of 1963, his election to executive leadership positions of the United Pentecostal Church International, and blazing innovative trails in multicultural ministries and metro evangelism.

Kenneth Mendenhall, pastor of Ironwood United Pentecostal Church in South Bend, Indiana, knew Willie Johnson well. He saw her in her home, visited her son's home, and she lived for a time in his house.

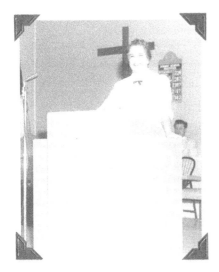

Sister Willie in the pulpit of Morningside Church, South Bend, Indiana, pastored by Kenneth Mendenhall.

"I often told her," said Mendenhall, "'Willie, don't get a chapter and try to explain it. You just sing and then talk. Sing and talk. That's how your ministry is.'

"She wore a long, full, white dress, and she would have a dark cape. When she got going real good, she'd just take that cape and twirl it around and preach. God used her in a mighty way.

"Before I was in the ministry, I went to see her one time at the old Morningside Church. The place was full. It was a small church. I took two of my friends with me. She was singing away and talking about getting close to God and she

---

87   As recorded in *Pioneer Pentecostal Women.*
88   Per Jack Yonts's daughter, Kathy Lemke.

pointed. She didn't know me from Adam. She pointed to us three and said, 'And I mean you three boys back there.'

"Later, when I was pastoring a small church out by Notre Dame, we had her there. Then we moved to the Indiana Avenue church and had her there. The move of God would be so much she would come to me and ask, 'Who do you want to come to the altar?' She would sing and go to that person, and they would automatically come while she was singing."

Sherry Weldy, a member of Kenneth Mendenhall's church, heard Sister Willie minister there. In fact, Sister Willie also ministered with Sherry's mother-in-law, Dorothy Weldy, in Middlebury, Indiana. She said Sister Willie's favorite saying was, "If God loves you, He'll cross your path," and she remembered her singing, "God Leads Us Along."

Lavona Sauters of West Virginia shared her memories of Sister Willie:

"I always knew her. She wound up at my grandmother's house and became acquainted with my family when my mom was still single. Sister Willie was staying with the preacher and his family, and we were having revival at 25th Street Church. My mom told me she got off the bus from work and heard someone playing the piano. There was Sister Willie at the piano. She knew my parents very well.

"When she was at 25th Street Church, we visited. We went to her revivals. She preached with such conviction, and she could stop in the middle of her sermon and point out somebody and tell something they needed in their life.

"'I got the Holy Ghost when I was eleven years old. I went to public school, and there were times I was weak, and I would desire to do the things others did, like being a majorette. But I couldn't wear the uniform. I thought I could be a cheerleader, but when I'd start to think about doing things like that I would remember what Sister Willie told me. I would remember, and it drew me back to where I needed to be with the Lord.

"I still sing her songs. I could put her records on right now, and I'd begin to well up and cry. I miss her. I wish I could see her again.

"I remember she had come back to 25th Street, and I knew she was going to be there. I wanted her to meet my husband and three children. I introduced her, and she hugged each one of them.

"'I wanted you to see my family,' I told her, 'how it turned out.'

"She said, 'Honey, it's turned out great.'

"I didn't know her all that well and didn't spend that much time with her, but I felt she was my friend. I'm sure thousands of other people felt the same way. She impacted our lives."

In 1949, Donald Haymon's family joined Pastor Lewis Manuwal in Northumberland, Pennsylvania, to help him establish a new church, Calvary Tabernacle. While the church was being built, the pastor conducted services in a tent. Sister Willie Johnson was the evangelist at their first tent revival, and it was through her ministry the church gained the needed foothold to propel the building project forward. Donald Haymon recalled with appreciation Sister Willie's incredible ministering ability in those services. She was an "accomplished pianist," said Haymon. "She sang with such zest, power, and anointing, that saints and sinners alike were moved to tears!"

Harold Aikey also recalled Sister Willie preaching for Pastor Manuwal. "I'm one of the few left here," he said. "She was a great evangelist."[89]

Larry Neal's family belonged to the First Pentecostal Church in the New Castle, Indiana, under the pastorship of Earl McElhaney. The family first came to the Lord when Larry was nine months old and after the passing of his older sister. "Sister Willie preached the night my aunt Nina repented," said Neal. "When she finished preaching, she turned to my pastor and said, 'I just caught you a big fish,' and that was my aunt.[90]

"My mother repented under the preaching of Sister Marie McElhaney. My father was an addicted, drinking gambler—smoked

---

89   Comment made in 2015 when Harold Aikey was 89 years old.

90   Nina Neal was a 67-year member of the United Pentecostal Church International, where she held many positions: teacher, youth leader, secretary-treasurer, trustee and others. She wrote the book, *Keepers of the Flame*, on the church's local history in New Castle, Indiana.

all the time. He grew up in a non-churched family. That was before the revival opened.

"She came every year. She was like a circuit rider. She had certain churches that were her churches. They were home to her, and she had many spiritual adopted children. I was with Sister Willie almost every year of my life growing up. Generally, she would come through our way about the first or second week of May. We had Saturday night street meetings at 6:00 p.m., and we would invite the people to be with us in service.

"James Rupe was in his seventies and a fresh widower. He came in grief to hear Sister Willie sing. She preached and gave the altar call. She walked the aisles that night and reached a point where she addressed old Mr. Rupe. 'Dad,' she said, 'won't you come and repent tonight and get saved?' He did. He was baptized and received the Holy Ghost and died suddenly of a natural death two weeks later.

"Sister Whipple was a Nazarene pastor's wife in Indianapolis who dared come hear 'this woman sing.' The revival was on at Brother Petty's. Sister Whipple received the Holy Ghost and went home speaking in tongues. She returned bringing Brother Whipple. He, too, received the Holy Ghost. It cost them the church they pastored, but Brother Whipple spent the rest of his life ministering from the Bible Church platform."

Revival in Indianapolis, 1946.

Sister Willie with Isabelle Wirick in Kokomo, Indiana, picture provided by Lois Truman

Rev. Willie Johnson, evangelist, who did much to organize the work of the Open Door Apostolic Mission, and whose efforts will always be deeply appreciated by Rev. Entsminger and his staff.

Open Door Article, 1940s.

NEW CASTLE, IND.

We are glad to report that Jesus is still working here. July 8, Elder Intsminger of Charleston, W. Va., was with us in a tent meeting at which unusually large crowds were present. During this meeting nine were baptized in Jesus' Name and two received the Holy Ghost.

One week later we started a three weeks' meeting with Evangelist Willie Johnson of Charleston, W. Va., during which 14 were baptized in Jesus' name and three filled with the Holy Ghost. Our church was packed every night and at some services the people could not get in.

On August 17, at 7:30 P.M., we burned the mortgage on our church. Elder W. T. Witherspoon of Columbus, Ohio, preached the message to a packed house. We were privileged to have the mayor of our city speak a few words for us that night.

Our fellowship meeting held on August 25 was a great success. God is still healing in our midst and blessing in a mighty way. Pray for us.

Pastor Earl McElhaney
Reporter Marie McElhan[...]

COMING!

OLD FASHIONED

TENT MEETING

14th and BRANCH STREET

BEGINNING
SATURDAY, JUNE 5th
SERVICES NIGHTLY AT 8 O'CLOCK
EXCEPT MONDAY

SPONSORED BY

WHITE WAY TABERNACLE

BLAIR & WARREN ST.

W. S. GUINN, Pastor

EVANGELIST
WILLIE JOHNSON
OF CHARLESTON, W. VA.

Revival with Pastor W. S. Guinn.

Pentecostal Outlook, September 1945, Publication of the Pentecostal Assemblies of Jesus Christ. Note reference to Bro. Entsminger.

I'm in Love with Jesus, and He's in Love with Me

Verse 1
Do you wonder why I'm happy
Do you wonder why I'm free
Well, the mighty God of heaven has laid His hand on me
He tells me not to worry
He'll supply my every need
Oh, I'm in love with Jesus, and He's in love with me

Refrain
Oh, I'm in love with Jesus, and He's in love with me
I've a picture of King Jesus that I want the world to see
He's the healer of all diseases
He's the master of the seas
Oh, I'm in love with Jesus, and He's in love with me

Verse 2
I was sad and lonely
I was poor as could be
'Til someone came and told me
The master calms the sea
I lifted my head in wonder
King Jesus was reaching for me
Oh, I'm in love with Jesus, and He loves me [91]

---

91 Author unknown.

Chapter 6:

I'M IN LOVE WITH JESUS, AND HE'S IN LOVE WITH ME

Music Ministry

S ister Willie was a talented musician and singer. Music was an integral part of her ministry, and there was never a service that she didn't sing.[92] She played the piano beautifully, and also played the guitar and tambourine.

Sister Willie playing
guitar, picture
used in songbook
published 1954.

---

92 Per David White.

"She was probably the classiest tambourine player that ever lived."

—James Stark

"Man, she could beat that tambourine."

—Teresa Schanzer

"She loved that tambourine."

—Daniel Scott

"I remember watching Sister Willie play her tambourine as she walked back and forth on the platform singing," said Neva Limones. "She didn't try to be perfect, but her songs came from deep down."

Evangelist Lee Stoneking said Sister Willie sang as led by the Holy Ghost, and the songs she sang under the anointing often set people free or brought liberty in the service.[93]

Sister Willie ministered in Sacramento when Jan Reavis was a young girl. "I will always remember her and that powerful voice she had," said Reavis. "I sing her songs to this day! God blessed Sister Willie with quite a ministry. She was amazing."

"Willie had substance," said Bob Gilstrap. "She didn't rely on emotion and getting people high, but they loved her ministry. Singing was such a part of her. I remember:

> *Lest I forget Gethsemane*
> *Lest I forget Thine agony*
> *Lest I forget Thy love for me*
> *Lead me to Calvary.[94]*

"We would sing that over and over and over," said Gilstrap, "and this:

---

93 Per Shaun Butler who heard this in a message spoken by Lee Stoneking.
94 "Lead Me to Calvary" by Jennie E. Hussey, 1921.

Billows may roll
The breakers may dash
But I shall not sway because
He holds me fast
So dark the day
Clouds in the sky
But I know it's alright
Because Jesus is nigh." [95]

Jimmy Ramsey noted with a chuckle how Sister Willie interjected a musical stop sign when people were gossiping. "She'd sing 'Just Go and Tell Jesus on Me,' and that would stop them in their tracks."

Just Go and Tell Jesus on Me

If from the presence of Jesus I stray
And my fall you happen to see
Remember it's best, if I fell by the way
To just go and tell Jesus on me
Just go and tell Jesus on me
Whatever my weakness may be
If you are my brother, don't go tell another
Just go and tell Jesus on me [96]

In 1964, Debby Harrah's family returned to the Open Door church after living for a time in California. "I had been taking piano lessons and then started filling in on the organ at Open Door about age fourteen," said Harrah. "Sister Day often took a break when Sister Willie was at home. So, when Sister Willie preached at Open Door, she would use the church musicians to play for her. Well, I had watched how Sister Day did it, so I did my best!

---

95 "My Soul Has Been Anchored" words and music by Douglas Miller (1904–1982), copyright date unknown.
96 Author unknown.

"Sister Willie was encouraging, and I stepped in, backing her soulful preaching. I loved it and could feel the anointing, myself.

"When you played when she was preaching, it meant you were on that organ bench playing before service, during song service, then during her singing and preaching, and then you played on through altar service. I learned so much under the ministry of Sister Willie Johnson that followed me in my life of music ministry.

"I learned to 'feel after the Spirit,' and God would bring to my mind the right song for the direction He wanted to go in. I learned to listen close, to be ready and spontaneous, because she would break out in song. It may be one that you didn't know or a chorus that she just created as she was preaching.

"You could feel the special anointing that she had and the response of the people. So I learned to just go with her. It might be a rejoicing song like 'The Church Way Out on the Hill' or it might be a deeper song like 'Submission' or 'He Washed My Eyes with Tears.'

"Among her many gifts, Sister Willie had the gift of discernment and the gift of knowledge that God would use during her preaching. She would go out in the congregation and minister to those God directed her to. I was privileged to play for her when she came to Open Door on and off until about 1972. I cherish those early years."

Darrell McBride also had the privilege to play the piano for Sister Willie several times. "She was truly anointed of God," he said. "Her ministry was heartfelt and heartwarming. Sister Johnson was a spiritual lady with great discernment, greatly used of God." Larry Neal added, "When you played for Sister Willie, you had to be ready to go anywhere, with any key, and any song or tempo. She made sharp 90 degree turns—from singing to preaching to deep weeping to glorious dancing."

"When a service was dragging and she thought it needed to pick up, she'd start singing, 'The Lord Saved Me, Why Should I Be Bound?' Then she'd go into 'The Lord healed me' and 'He filled me with the Holy Ghost,' and literally

she could take a service that seemed like it was twice
dead, plucked up by the roots, and people would be totally
enraptured in the Holy Ghost when she finished singing."

—James Stark

"She had a song sheet," said Larry Neal. "She sold them for
maybe 15 cents back in the day. She would sell a few things. People
wanted something from her. That's why the picture you have on the
front of your book was on cardstock, and she sold that for 15–20
cents. It was memorable to the many, many people she influenced in
her ministry."

Sister Willie recorded one 78 RPM single record. One side was
"If I Can Just Make it In," and the second, "I Know Who Holds
Tomorrow." She recorded three full-length 33 RPM albums. One
was made in Stockton, California, and Kenneth Haney, who went on
to be the General Superintendent of the United Pentecostal Church
International, was one of the background singers.[97]

Album titles:
1. *I Trust in God*
2. *I Thank the Lord*
3. *Through the Waters*

Dan Scott digitized Sister Willie's records to make it possible for
people today to be moved by her ministry of song.[98]

---

97 Per James Stark.
98 Visit *www.affirmingfaith.org* to listen to Sister Willie sing the songs on her albums as
well as other audio recordings.

Dear Friends,

Hymns are not sung with the voice alone, they are sung with the heart and soul.

Willie Johnson has the heart, the soul and to make the combination complete, a magnificent voice. All over the states, she is recognized as one of the truly inspirational singers of hymns and gospel songs. Her dynamic interpretations of sacred music are soul-stirring examples of reverence, depth, humility, devotion and artistry.

There is a hymn or gospel for every conceivable emotion. Some offer hope, assurance and comfort. Some are pure adoration, tenderness and love, others despair at a sinful world and the fall from grace.

There is jubilation and exaltation, glorification of God and the great promise to mankind. From a musical standpoint, there is nothing more intrinsically beautiful than sacred music. Free and natural melodies, soul-felt rhythms, moody harmonies, undeniable sincerity are the ingredients of truly fine music. They all exist in the great gospel song.

It is small wonder then, that their ideal presentation demands a superlative soul, heart and voice. To find these qualities in one person is a rare experience. That person, however, has been found! It is, without a doubt, Sister Willie Johnson.

30 years of preaching and thousands of miles traveled in the United States and Canada, her anointed, consec[...] ministry and singing has blessed many.

Upon your many requests, this second album has been [...] for your enjoyment and spiritual worship.

Backing Sister Johnson in several songs is WES[...] APOSTOLIC BIBLE COLLEGE CHOIR, Stockton, Reverend Kenneth Haney, Choir Director.

Charlene Day-Organist and Pianist, also travels with Johnson in all revival meetings.

Promotion for Album.

Promotion for Album by Apostolic Melodie Record Company, Bellflower, California.

I Trust in God

Sister Willie Johnson

Dear Friends;

Upon your many requests this album has been made, for your enjoyment and spiritual worship.

Sister Willie Johnson is a very capable and anointed singer and minister in the United Pentecostal Church. She has been preaching and singing this glorious truth for thirty years.

Countless thousands have heard and been blessed by her anointed singing and preaching.

She has traveled thousands of miles over the United States and Canada, preaching and singing the gospel.

Accompanying her in all her meetings is talented Charlene Day of Tulsa, Oklahoma, who has devoted her time and talent to the work of the Lord on the evangelistic field.

Sister Johnsons consecrated life and wonderful personality has won her many friends through the years.

Combined in this album are selected songs she felt would be a blessing to her many friends, such as My Thanks To Him, Not My Will, Grow Closer and I Trust in God, done in a slow spirit felt style, to the more jubilant hand clapping spirituals such as More than All, The Lord Will Make Away, and Since I Met Jesus, backed by the Tackett-Day Trio.

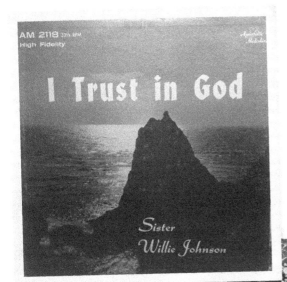

I Trust in God
album cover.

I Thank the Lord
album cover.

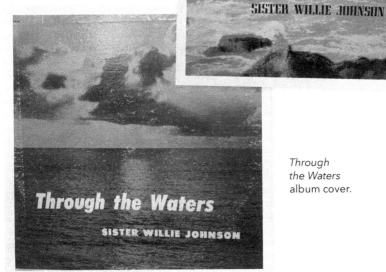

*Through
the Waters*
album cover.

Use Me

Verse 1
Use me, oh, Lord, use me
I am weak but Thou art strong
Take me in, oh, Lord, your sheltering arms
Then, oh, Lord, my Savior be
Use me, oh, Lord, use me

Refrain
I want you to pick, pick me up when I am down
Plant my feet right now on solid ground
Then, oh, Lord, thy servant I'll be
Use me, oh, Lord, use me[99]

---

99 Author unknown.

Chapter 7

USE ME

Team Ministry with Charlene Day

In the early years of Sister Willie's ministry, she most often traveled alone, but in the 1950s, she met a young woman who began accompanying her both on the road and on the organ. For over twenty years, Charlene Day had the right songs, and not only did she play, she sang, as well.[100] "It was powerful," said Daniel Scott. "Charlene would be so sensitive that Willie would break into a song to match her message, and how they would minister."

> "They traveled together. They were a wonderful team. They worked together. Charlene would play the organ or piano. Sister Willie's ministry was singing in the Spirit and using her songs to preach. That was how she did it. She wasn't any great pulpiteer to get a Scripture and give you a divine revelation, but she'd give you a Scripture, and then she'd start singing, and everybody loved her."
> —Kenneth Mendenhall

---

100 Per Kenneth Mendenhall.

SISTER WILLIE JOHNSON and
Co-Worker - CHARLENE DAY

Sister Willie and Charlene Day.

Sister Willie Johnson

Sister Willie with her tambourine.

According to her brother, Dan Day, Charlene met Sister Willie at a revival she was preaching at First Apostolic in West Tulsa. Sister Willie often ministered in the Tulsa church, and Charlene was attending the nearby Apostolic College.

Frank Glasco, Charlene's landlord in later years, believed, "They got together because during one of the ministry events, Sister Willie did not have a musician. Charlene, being the person she was, maybe volunteered or was present to act as her musician. They clicked. The bond was instant. She felt this was where God was leading her."

"Charlene had a heart condition," recalled Alice Torres, "and when Sister Willie was preaching, she told her if she would be baptized in Jesus's name, God would heal her. She did, and He did."

Charlene's parents belonged to an Assemblies of God church. When Charlene completed her program at the Bible school, she returned home and told her mom and dad she wanted to travel with Sister Willie. According to her brother, Charlene's parents were "ok with Charlene going." He said they understood her reasons, but their mother "missed her a lot."

Dan Day also deeply missed his sister. "I was extremely sad when she left," said Day. "She was always nosy in my business. If I ever needed to know anything, I would just ask her, because she knew everything. But I missed her, and I loved her very much."

Charlene Day was petite and had a very kind heart. She also had an adventurous streak and was always willing to try new things.[101] "She was a pistol," her brother said. "Charlene had a personality you wouldn't believe. She was always wound up like an eight-day clock on a seven-day stretch. She was always into things as far as moving around and active."

According to Day, Charlene loved to play the piano, and she could also play a stand-up bass, accordion, and organ. In her younger years, she had been a disciplined piano student, but later when she began playing church music, she would listen to the music and was able to play the songs by ear.[102]

"She had talent," said Glasco. She mentioned her mother sent her to take piano lessons in elementary school. "She didn't like the lady who was her teacher," said Glasco, "and she didn't like the kind of music she was teaching. She always had an ear for gospel and that kind of music."

Charlene and Sister Willie bee-lined around the United States. "They traveled to New Mexico, New York, Michigan, and Texas," said Glasco. "Charlene met up with people in the churches, and she was the organist

---

101 Per Dan Day.
102 Per Dan Day and Frank Glasco.

for one of the big black community churches for a long time. They called her 'the dot at the end of the fence' because she was white."

"She was very talented," said Day. "She could play gospel music for the black community, and she played that organ for that choir. She traveled right with them on the bus. She traveled with that group for three or four years, and it took two Greyhound buses to fit the choir, but then she went back with Sister Willie."

Sister Willie stayed several times in the Day's home. "She was a wonderful lady," said Day. "We really loved Sister Willie. She was an angel on earth. That's all there is to it."

> "Charlene would come with Sister Willie and stay in our home. I'd play some for Sister Willie as far as altar service, and I would be on the piano or organ when Charlene was playing. We enjoyed each other on the keyboard."
>
> —Bob Gilstrap

> "In the '50s and '60s, Sister Willie traveled with Charlene Day. It was very special. Sister Willie's singing was very powerful. When she showed up, it was just incredible. We had breakthroughs. It was very reviving."
>
> —David Fauss

After Charlene moved to Houston, she told Frank Glasco about a time she had been forced to face her fears on the road. Sister Willie's travel itinerary had required the women to cross the Golden Gate Bridge, and Charlene had been afraid. The thought of driving across the one-mile suspension bridge scared her. "It was something she was not mentally prepared to do," said Glasco, "but she did all the driving. So drive across it, she did."

Charlene did more than drive and play the organ. She assisted Sister Willie and took care of her.[103] For many years the two lived and traveled together. Charlene managed their schedule and the details of their travel. That, at times, proved challenging, as it was said that Sister Willie was seldom bound by clock or calendar.[104]

Daniel Scott provided some insight.

"Charlene kept her schedule the best she could, but Sister Willie did not always give notice if she decided to stay. Lots of times I received calls from pastors across the country asking, 'Where is she? She is supposed to be here.'

"I would ask, 'Why do you want to know?' (I wouldn't tell them she is in such and such a place.)

"They would say, 'She was supposed to have started a revival for me tonight.'

"And I would say, 'You will hear from Charlene, and you will have to understand, Sister Willie will follow the will of God regardless.'

"One superintendent got bizarrely out of sorts. I told Sister Willie about it, and I happened to be in a special district meeting where Willie and that superintendent were there. She went straight to him. I was standing there.

"She said, 'Brother, it's a good thing I didn't come to the church, because if I had come, it would've wasted our time and God's time with an attitude like you have.'"

Daniel Scott served as a barrier for Sister Willie. Some pastors who were delayed or cancelled were not happy, which was understandable, since they had advertised and prepared and there had been great expectation of her coming.

"They had no channel of communication except my wife, Joy, and me," said Scott. "They at times expressed their anger, and it was my job to bridge the gap. I usually used their church as a reason. I'd say, 'If she was

---

103 Per Frank Glasco and James Stark.
104 As recorded in *Pioneer Pentecostal Women*.

with you and God was doing a special work, would you want her to leave you? Let's allow God to direct Willie, and when your meeting begins with her, your spirit and attitude will honor you with a successful meeting.'"

"Pastors would go to General Conference to see if they could get Sister Willie to go to their church directly after. They would try to get her to come back with them just to be sure they had her."[105]

—James Stark

Sister Willie's apparent disorganization as far as schedule and other details of life frustrated many, but it was the same "live in the moment" approach to life[106] that enabled her to follow the leading of the Spirit in ministry.

"Willie Johnson showed me something, and I don't know that it could ever be copied. She had her way of just helping the people to be relaxed and free in the Spirit. She was herself, and she would be this way and that way and talking to you and looking right at you and walking out to the audience on a very personal level, ministering and laying hands. She loved to talk in tongues, talk in tongues, talk in tongues.

"What it taught me is we have our own style. Willie's type of ministering could teach all of us when to just 'let go and let God.'

"I asked her about that. I said, 'I have one question. What happens if I should try to minister like you're doing but the people aren't responding? They aren't really flowing? They aren't really crying or worshiping?'

---

105 On a side note, Sister Willie confided to Allen Donham that she never liked to preach at large conferences.
106 James Stark used the phrase "live in the moment."

"She said, 'Well, fine. Just preach them a straight message. Just give them the Word of God.'

"That taught me if the Spirit starts to move, go with that. Let the Lord move and do what He wants to do and have a shouting or crying time or whatever God is doing to get people close to Him or get the Holy Ghost. If they're not in that mood—if they're just kind of straight-laced—be prepared to give them a good message, and the Word of the Lord will not return void."

—Allen Donham

Charlene was single and 29 years younger than her companion. Sister Willie reportedly attempted to add matchmaking to her résumé. "The last time or two Sister Willie preached for me in Denver," said Donald Haymon, "she tried to match me up with her traveling partner, Charlene Day."

Dan Day did not know the details of how Sister Willie and Charlene's paths separated. He believed Sister Willie became ill and Charlene ended up in Houston with friends. Frank Glasco said Charlene moved to Houston in the 1970s, and at that time, the traveling ministry of the duo was over. He believed it was due to Sister Willie's health and inability to continue traveling full-time.

"I tried to get her to come home," said her brother, "but she decided to stay in Houston. My mother would have welcomed her back; my dad, too, any time. She was in business with a man named Frank for a while. She was in a travel agent-type business for a while, and she had a recipe from my great-great-great-grandmother for chocolates and brittle, and she was in that business. She sold her candies to the councilmen, mayor, and other people. She put together a recipe for jalapeno brittle, too."

Dan Day attended several revival services with Sister Willie and Charlene. "I loved their ministry," he said. "Sister Willie would be preaching and all of a sudden break into a song. Charlene would pick up on it, and away they would go. It would be fascinating the way it happened.

"I remember one song she sang:

"Peace, peace, wonderful peace coming down from the Father above."

Chris Sowards remembered Charlene accompanying Sister Willie when she ministered in Charleston. "Charlene used to come and play the organ," said Sowards. "She lived in Texas, but came in several times and played." When Charlene was not able to be with Sister Willie, Sowards's mother accompanied her. "When my mom played," said Sowards, "Sister Willie would say, 'Put the gravy on.' That came from the black church."

Charlene Day paid a great price to minister full-time on the road with Sister Willie, but as her brother Dan testified, "She was giving her best for the Lord."

Hold to God's Unchanging Hand

Verse 1
Time is filled with swift transition
Naught of earth unmoved can stand
Build your hopes on things eternal
Hold to God's unchanging hand

Refrain
Hold to God's unchanging hand
Hold to God's unchanging hand
Build your hopes on things eternal
Hold to God's unchanging hand

Verse 2
Trust in Him who will not leave you
Whatsoever years may bring
If by earthly friends forsaken
Still more closely to Him cling

Verse 3
When your journey is completed
If to God you have been true
Fair and bright the home in glory
Your enraptured soul will view[107]

---

107 Sister Willie did her own rendition of this song which was written by Jennie Wilson and edited by John E. Thomas in 1906. Music by Franklin L. Eiland. Public Domain.

Chapter 8

HOLD TO GOD'S UNCHANGING HAND

The 1950s

In the 1950s, Sister Willie's ministry was in full swing. Her revivals played an important part in establishing a new work launched in 1950 in Sutton, West Virginia. She preached revival meetings in the early days of this new work pastored by Wilford Blake. In fact, in the Spring of 1951, after the church acquired a tent, Sister Willie held the first revival meeting in the tent. The *Pentecostal Herald* reported, "God moved in a marvelous way."[108]

Teresa Schanzer recalled memories of annual January revivals in Charleston:

"I was like nine years old, and she would have these revivals. When you're in school, all you think about is going home and going to bed. We wouldn't get out until 11:00 at night.

"Her car broke down one time up some hollow. We were sitting in the car freezing while my dad went to work on her car and got her home. It was pouring down snow and all I wanted to do was go home and go to bed.

"But I remember even at nine years old (and usually kids that age aren't interested in preaching), but she always kept me interested. I listened

---

108 The *Pentecostal Herald*, October 1951, page 13, reported by Justine Wamer.

to every word she said. I remember her pacing across the platform. She always wore that white uniform with a black cape, and when she swung her arm around it was white silk inside—it would show that white.

"And she would always sing songs. She would always preach about 'some through the water.' That was almost like her motto song. She would sing 'Down from His Glory.' She sang so good. I just loved Sister Willie."

Dave Ramsey also remembered his father working on Sister Willie's car. "Dad was a body man and worked on Sister Willie's '65 Cadillac. She liked red so much she wanted it painted from light green to red.

"When she lived in Sissonville, we would go out to her house frequently, and my dad would buy her a bucket of chitlins and take it to her. We never ate chitlins, but he would always buy them for her because she loved them."

In 1952, Glen Leaman, who pastored the Apostolic Gospel Church in Crooksville, Ohio, wanted to have Sister Willie minister at his church. His son, Jack, recalled the details, "We lived in a little town, and there were not supposed to be any black people there. My dad felt to have her preach, so he went to the mayor, got permission, and she preached a revival for us. It was outstanding. She was really very anointed.

"She stayed with us, and it was very interesting to have her stay in our home. She was quite a lady, a very good singer, a good preacher, and she had very good results in her ministry."[109]

> "When I was just a kid my dad pastored the church in Skiatook, Oklahoma. Sister Willie came several times to our church over the years and preached revivals for us. She stayed in our home, so we became very, very close to Willie Johnson.
>
> "My dad's church was small. We ran 100–110, and Sister Willie was the only evangelist that could come to our church and pack the building out. We would have revivals

---

109 Scottie Johnson (Sister Willie's son) also preached in Crooksville, Ohio, according to Jack Leaman.

and announce them and have a few visitors; but when we announced her, it would be full.

"She would preach for the Ashcrafts who pastored in Oklahoma, and they were close friends to my mom and dad. I called her Aunt Ila and him Uncle Joe. We grew up as if they were part of our family, but there was no kin.

"We were down there visiting the revival. I was a young teenager, and I went into a big room to change clothes. As I was putting my britches on (I don't know if it was her bedroom or just a room), she opened the door and said, 'Boy, get your britches on!' She was just a part of our family. We were so close.

"I remember we were out. We were fishing—or someone told us about this—but she was out fishing in a boat and got hungry. She opened her purse and pulled out a chicken drumstick. Somewhere they had stopped and eaten and she had probably stuck an extra drumstick in her purse."

—Bob Gilstrap

Revival, Skiatook, Oklahoma, 1950

Gracie Mitchell laughed as she remembered how much Sister Willie loved chicken. "She loved to eat, and she loved fried chicken," said Gracie. "We always went in Dayton to a chicken place, and we got her as much as she could eat. Of course, we ate also, but she would take whatever was left, wrap it in a napkin, and put it in her purse. She'd say, 'I'll eat this later. I will.' And she did. She liked Chinese, too."

Sister Willie was a dear friend of Robert and Gracie Mitchell, and she made a significant impact on Robert Mitchell's preaching ministry. "When we first met her," said Gracie, "I was very young. It was in my home church in Houston. She was there at Reverend C. L. Dees's church. We heard her preach and sing. Singing was mostly her ministry, but she would call people out and go pray for people.

"She came to my husband and I at that first meeting. She talked to him about his sermons and what he was going to preach. He was surprised. He'd had his call, but he hadn't started preaching. She talked to me also—that I have a calling. And the first time I ever was asked to speak, I called her. She said, 'You're going to go, and you're going to do fine.'"

Larry Neal recalled Sister Willie's account of the first revival she preached at Pastor Dees's church. "It was one of the more elaborate buildings," said Neal. "It was red brick with white, columned pillars. It had red carpeting, white-on-dark oak pews, and a fountain in the lobby. She preached a few services, and she didn't really have the freedom that she wanted. In one of the services, she got to the point she kicked her shoes off. It was like a release, and then she really went in 'the mode.' It was great. It just set the service. She dropped all the formalities."

"Back in the '50s, Sister Willie came to Riverside Apostolic," said Allen Donham. "I was seven years old, and there were 50 who received the Holy Ghost. This was no doubt one of many milestones."

Kenneth Morgan recalled Sister Willie as "a wonderful and delightful person" who meant so much to him and his wife. "I first heard this dear and precious lady when I was a teenager in Apostolic

College in Tulsa, Oklahoma," recalled Morgan. "When I was later called to the ministry and became the pastor of the First Pentecostal Church in Groves, Texas, Sister Willie Johnson came and preached us a revival. When she preached, we consistently had the largest crowds of any revival in the church while I was pastor there.

"Sister Willie Johnson had a commanding presence about her everywhere she went. She drew and captivated people's attention as though they perceived they were in the presence of greatness when they were around her. She made people believe in themselves whether they were in a church service or when she traveled on the train.

"She often stopped and turned to someone who was weeping in the service and quietly ministered to their brokenness, and then went right back to her thought. She did that several times in a service, and by the time she gave the altar appeal, the altar filled up with people who were desperate to invite God into their lives."

A Miracle Report from John Bernardini

"Sister Willie used to come to Orange, Texas, and hold a revival every year. When I was a small boy, five years old, I had rheumatic fever. In the '50s that was a serious disease that killed a lot of small children. For several months, I had to be given penicillin shots four to five times a week to keep my fever at 101. The doctors said if I lived, I would have damage to my heart. She prayed for me, and I was instantly healed. God instantly healed me, and there was no damage to my heart. The doctors could not believe what had happened.

"She came back to Orange when I was twelve years old. Fred Foster was the pastor then. Apparently, she picked up the calling God had already put on my life. She said, 'I am going to impart into you gifts that I have,' and then she prayed for me. I went completely unconscious and stayed unconscious for a long time.

"As I got older and began to minister myself, God gave me the gift of discernment and also the gift of faith. My mother, Shirley Bernardini, also had the gift of faith. Sister Willie would call her when she was within a 50-mile radius to ask her to pray for people who needed deliverance. They were very close."

Adrian Stanley also recalled Sister Willie ministering in Orange, Texas. She was a "dear woman of God," said Stanley, and she "preached a revival people are still talking about today."[110]

David White's grandfather, W. T. Poling, pastored in Morgantown from the 1930s to the 1960s. "She would come every year for revival," said White. "I was probably four or five years old the first time I remember her coming. She would come and stay in the house with us the whole time. I've known her probably all my life. We were in Morgantown, and she was in Charleston. She was a fixture every year at the church.

Morgantown, West Virginia. We are glad to report a wonderful revival meeting of three weeks duration at our church in Norwood Addition of Morgantown in which fourteen repented of their sins, were baptized in the name of the Lord Jesus and 12 received the baptism of the Holy Ghost. Much good was also accomplished among other people in the church. We were privileged to have Evangelist Willie Johnson of Charleston, West Virginia, who was a real blessing to us and was greatly used of God in the services. She will be of great help to any Pastor. We are thankful for this good meeting.

H. I. Goodin, Pastor.

Pentecostal Herald, February 1950.

---

110 As told by Stanley in 2010.

Morgantown Post, February 8, 1958.

"She loved to go uptown and shop. She always drove a big car. One day she parked it in the street and locked her keys inside. When she got back to the vehicle and couldn't get in, she knew the keys were inside. A policeman saw her and went over to ask her what the problem was. He got tools and opened the door. She was very boisterous, and after he got her in, she said, 'Thank you, Jesus!'

"The policeman said, 'Don't thank Jesus. Thank me. I'm the one who opened your door.'

"My grandad had a fairly large church for a Pentecostal church—300 or better. When she came, it would take every chair. We would have to go to the funeral home and get chairs and load the basement with speakers and chairs. Kids would sit on the altar and in the windows because there was no other place to sit. The church was packed. She drew crowds.

"I remember I was on the board for the Women's Aglow. She was in town, and there were two or three ladies there involved who got her to speak for the Women's Aglow. It's a good organization, but she brought a power that day into that place they had never seen before— something we had demonstrated in the Apostolic church for years—but these women were mostly from a liturgical background. They had never seen the anointing in that fashion.

"In the Aglow meeting she talked, 'Now do you want to know how I was baptized?'

"They all nodded their heads, yes.

"She told them and explained why. I don't know how many of those ladies within the next four or five months I baptized. They didn't leave their church, but I baptized several of them in Jesus's name, and I think it was all because of her sharing her experience.

"When my grandfather had ministers in for revivals, none of them stayed in hotels. They all stayed at the house, and every night after church we went to the house and my grandmother fixed an evening meal. We would sit at the dining room table, and they would tell stories and the things that happened in their ministries. That was just a part of what went on. It didn't matter if it was Sister Willie or someone else. What was funny, there was always one night somewhere during the week or two or three or four weeks of revival they would tell ghost stories. I always got a kick out of the ghost stories.

"Sister Willie might just be passing through, and she would stop at our house and stay. She would just open the door and come in. It was her home. She was part of the family."

Another account from Morgantown came from Margaret Krider. "Sister Willie had an impression on everyone who met her," she said. "In 1951, my little girl drowned, and she was able to minister to my loss because of her loss."

David and Monte Showalter received the Holy Ghost in 1959 at Calvary Apostolic Church during a revival preached by Sister Willie. David said, "There were a few more that received the Holy Ghost during that revival. I just remember the services were very good, even for us as young boys."

Lorraine Ziemke attended a revival service at Calvary Apostolic Church in Omaha, Nebraska, on May 6, 1956. Her family had traveled thirty miles from their home to the church Lorraine's uncle, Jerry Tiller, pastored.

"She would get to preaching and jump off of the platform," said Lorraine, "and that cape would fly up. I was fourteen years old . . . and was seeking for the Holy Ghost with evidence of speaking in tongues. After each service, I went to the altar to pray.

"One Sunday, I stayed after morning service with my Grandma Tiller. Uncle Wallace offered to bring me home after evening service. That night, I prayed at the altar. Surely I wouldn't get the Holy Ghost tonight, I thought, because my mom wasn't there. Still, each time I prayed, I felt I would be that much closer to receiving it. I just relaxed and praised God. It wasn't long before I was speaking in tongues, a beautiful heavenly language. It was so enjoyable to feel so blessed of God. I was excited to tell my family."

"Sister Willie was a mighty preacher," recounted Vesta Mangun. She recalled a time Sister Willie preached in Indianapolis and she called out a young lady. Sister Mangun remembered Sister Willie saying, "You little dancing girl—you will change your dancing shoes tonight!"

At the age of 91, Margaret Martin, the "dancing girl," still vividly remembered the details of her encounter with Sister Willie Johnson. "I was going to be a Hawaiian dancer and a singer," said Martin. "My mother did not want me in the theatrical world. She told me, 'There's a lady out in a church who sings the blues, Margie, like you do. I'd like you to go hear her.'

"I said, 'Well, Mom, I guess I could go with you one night, but when they start that altar call stuff, I'm leaving.'

"When we got in the church, I'd never been there before or met or seen Willie Johnson. I knew no one in that church. My mother and I walked in. I was interested in Sister Willie's singing. She sang kind of like the blues.[111] Then she started preaching, and somewhere in the middle of her preaching, she stopped and said, 'God has changed my message, and I've got to change.'

---

111 Margaret's daughter, Mary Wilson, said Sister Willie's singing reminded her of Mahalia Jackson.

"She came down off the platform. I'd never seen the woman before in my life, had never been in that church, and did not know anyone in that church.[112] Sister Willie came down the aisle, pointed her finger straight at me and said, 'Dancing girl, throw away those dancing slippers.' And the message was directly for me.

"I hit the altar. I knew nothing about the church. My dad was against Oneness people—said they were of the devil. All I knew was what I felt. I ended up in the baptismal tank.

"Right after that (it was back in the wartime), I was going to be a USO entertainer, and I had struck up a relationship with the trombone player in the orchestra. I went back and told him, 'I can't do this anymore. I joined a church.'

"He said, 'I don't believe that. I can't believe it. I'm going to go to that church.'

"He came with me. I was so engrossed with my experience, and he kept watching me. He said, 'I don't understand it, but it has to be something real because it has sure changed you.'"

Many people who shared memories of Sister Willie had only vague recollections from childhood. One was Nancy Starkey. Starkey said when she was ten years old, she and her father "both accepted the Lord during her revival in 1957 in Chesapeake, Virginia."

Tammy Wilson also remembered Sister Willie from a child's vantage point. "I do remember wanting to be like her when I grew up," said Wilson. "The relationship she had with God was very powerful, and her anointing was evident."

Maurice DeFord recalled two revivals Sister Willie preached in his home church, Zion Tabernacle in Frankfort, Indiana. "She prayed a remarkably prophetic prayer over me during one altar service."

---

112 Mary Wilson shared that Margaret had at first been upset with her mother because she believed she had spoken to Sister Willie about her dancing before coming to the service.

DeFord also fondly remembered a time Sister Willie ministered at Saberton Apostolic Church in Morgantown. "She approached Janet Spiker (a visitor that evening) during the altar service," said DeFord, "and she asked her, 'Have you received the Holy Ghost?' Janet said, 'No,' and Sister Johnson laid her hand on her head, and Janet received the Holy Ghost."[113]

This event was significant to DeFord, because Janet went on to attend and graduate from Apostolic Bible Institute in 1961, and she afterwards became Mrs. Maurice DeFord.

Larry Neal, also from Indiana, recalled how beloved Sister Willie was to the members of the church in New Castle. "Our church loved Sister Willie so much they just couldn't do enough for her," said Neal. "When she would come, the people who lived on the farm would bring her freshly churned butter in Ball fruit jars. She could put her order in.

"Sometimes when she was here in the '50s, Sister Golder (whose husband, Morris, pastored a Pentecostal Assemblies of the World church in Indianapolis) would take her to Indianapolis during the day. Some people didn't like it because they thought they were wearing her out.

"She was holding revival here and was having heart trouble. She had been diagnosed with heart trouble, and she began to read the paper. Every day she found somebody locally here in the paper that died of heart trouble—every day. It was really testing her faith because she was sick and she was preaching. It reached a point where she told our pastor, 'I'm really getting weakened with this heart trouble.' We had lots of healings in those days, and he just simply laid his hand on her, anointed her head, and God healed her instantly of heart trouble. I heard her give that testimony in Houston."

Neal also told of the many times Sister Willie sang on the lawn of the Henry County courthouse. "Men sat in second- and third-floor windows mesmerized by her anointed voice and ministering words,"[114] said Neal. "Gamblers dropped their cards to come from taverns down

---

113 DeFord recalled this as being in 1956. He said the couple married in 1962 and served together in ministry for over 45 years.
114 The buildings were offices for attorneys, doctors, dentists, and insurance agents; and also hotel rooms, according to Larry Neal.

the street to stand and listen at a distance. Years after she ministered in the street services, I would find people who, when they found out I was Pentecostal, they would always bring up 'that black lady that sang.' Her singing was so unforgettable, so powerful. She was so anointed.

"Saturday night brought the farmworkers to town. Paul and Emily Hatley and their children, Clyde and Lois came. They took in the 6:00 p.m. courthouse square street meeting and heard Sister Willie sing. They had come from Tennessee and never heard of Pentecostal. After the street meeting, they accepted the invitation to follow us back to the church for Saturday night revival service. The rest is history. Little nine-year-old Lois was the first to receive the baptism of the Holy Ghost. She danced nonstop like a glowing angel under the power of God. Awesome, innocent purity.

"Brother Harley was uneducated. He couldn't even read the Bible much, but he carried the long burden for my soul, and he tarried with me faithfully until I was thirteen. He would not give up, and he prayed me through to the Holy Ghost and fire!

"At age fifteen, I was the six-days-a-week stockboy for our city's finest home furnishings store. They carried china, crystal, custom drapery, carpeting, etc. I worked for the McCormicks . . . devout Catholics. Their store was on Broad Street, next to the bank, directly across the street from our Saturday 6:00 p.m. street meetings. For years later, Pete McCormick would reminisce and tell people about '*that* black lady.' He said, 'Nobody could sing like her. I couldn't work when she was singing!'"

James Stark recalled a time his mother, Ella May Stark, traveled with his aunt to North Carolina to visit his Uncle Paul who had leukemia. After visiting and leaving him at the Veterans hospital, Ella May decided on the way back through Charleston to see if Sister Willie was home. She was exhausted and drained and did not realize that she herself was ill.

Neither of the travelers had a phone number or address for Sister Willie. Her number was not listed, and it was late in the evening. The ladies drove into Charleston where they found a large fruit market open and began asking around.

Sister Willie's son Rudolph worked as a police officer in Charleston. They located his number in the directory, called it, and told him who they were. Rudolph gave them Sister Willie's phone number and then told them they were standing across the street from her house.

"She prayed for my mother," said Stark. "She did not know she had a malignancy they would find four months later. Sister Willie prayed for her; she assured her that God knew where she was and what was happening, and that He would bring her through.

"At the time I was a freshman in high school. Mother was 49, I believe, and she was diagnosed four months after that with colorectal cancer. She lived to be 83."

After her visit with Sister Willie that day in Charleston, Ella May Stark felt she was able to face what was coming. "Any woman who has suffered as she has," said Ella May, "and has endured without complaining as she has, is an inspiration to the rest of us to press on."[115]

Cynthia Roy remembered Sister Willie from a tent revival she held back in the '50s with her mother, Goldie Goddard. "They prayed a lot together and fasted," said Roy.

"Mom said before service Sister Willie would hide her Bible in the audience.[116] Then when she would make her appearance in the auditorium, she would start singing and swaying back and forth as she walked down the aisle. Sister Willie would sing, 'I'm looking for the stone that was hewn out of the mountain.'[117]

"She said Sister Johnson would sing loud and speak under the anointing, and then she would go and find her Bible. Then she would lean back and sing, 'I've found that stone that was hewn out of the mountain' and begin to shout down the aisle.

---

115 This account was told by James Stark and also recorded in *Pioneer Pentecostal Women*. The quote from Ella May Stark comes from the book.
116 Linda McGinnis also recounted Sister Willie hiding her Bible in services she attended.
117 Song title "Looking For the Stone" or "Daniel Saw the Stone," author unknown.

"Sister Willie didn't get to finish that revival at that time with my mother. Something happened about her husband, so she told my mother to finish it. Many received the Holy Ghost and were baptized."

Mary June Bruner heard Sister Willie minister late in the '50s. "I remember being very impressed with her and her uniform," said Bruner. "She held a revival in Fort Worth, Texas, when I was about eleven or twelve years old. I remember black women coming to hear her preach, and oh, how they could testify. I still remember one woman saying in her testimony, 'Jesus showed me who He were.'"

Other remarkable testimonies have followed in the wake of Sister Willie's ministry. Douglas Rashall remembered one incredible encounter that occurred in the late 1950s or early 1960s. "Sister Willie was preaching a revival in San Francisco," said Rashall. "A person who had it in mind to commit suicide was parked at the base of the Golden Gate Bridge and was going to jump but picked up a tract from where she was preaching. That person came to church that night and received the Holy Ghost."

Walter Guinn pastored the church at Blair and Warren Streets in St. Louis, Missouri.[118] Sister Willie began holding meetings for Pastor Guinn at this location before the church moved to Grand and Carter Streets where Guinn's granddaughter, Lois Truman, first heard Sister Johnson in the late 1950s.

"I was ten or twelve at the time," said Truman. "She would preach for my grandpa, and my uncle, Charles McClain, was the piano player for the church. She would preach, exhort, and she would sing. It just kind of flowed as she would present. No two services were the same.

"My parents, Robert and Margie McFarland, were missionaries, and we were overseas during a lot of this, but I do remember being in

---

118 This was the church where the merger took place between the former Pentecostal Church Incorporated and Pentecostal Assemblies of Jesus Christ to form the United Pentecostal Church International.

Grandpa's church on more than one occasion when she was there in revival. She would really build up the sanctuary. It was like she was just letting the Lord speak through her, and as the Spirit led, she would sing, and speak some more, and just minister to people. She would walk out in the congregation and pray for them. She was very mobile in her presentation.

"Grandpa was one of the first churches to have her in Missouri. It was always very miraculous when she was there. There was a sense of the miraculous in her presence.

"I used to sing her songs as a kid, and I tried to sound like her."

Charles McClain, Lois Truman's uncle and the piano player at the church in St. Louis referenced above, contributed his memories of Sister Willie's visits:

"The last visit she made (which was in the '60s or early '70s) was with Sister Charlene. Charlene played the organ for her and would also augment Sister Willie's exhorting with runs and sounds from the organ. The organ was *whoop whooping* when Sister Johnson spoke.

"Sister Johnson had always stayed in the Guinn's home, but the last trip with Sister Charlene they stayed in a basement apartment that was in the very nice home of the Evans family (members of the Guinn's church).

"Sister Willie talked about how mean her husband was at times— locking her out of the house when she went to church. She said she was on her way to the river to commit suicide when she walked past the Pentecostal church and went inside. That was her salvation."

The stay in the Evans's home was also documented by their granddaughter, Sandra Nicholson. "Sister Willie came for many years to Brother Walter Guinn's church where I was raised," said Nicholson. "She stayed a couple of times with my grandparents, Mahlon and Beatrice Evans, and during one of her prayer meetings at their home, they were filled with the Holy Ghost.

"After my grandparents passed away, Sister Willie and Sister Charlene stayed with my parents, and I would get to ride to church with them. Such wonderful memories."

Revival Services in Miami

"I was young, but I still have memories of Sister Willie preaching, singing and worshiping," said Wayne Herring. "When she wasn't in the pulpit (say during song service), she would sing with enthusiasm and play the tambourine.

"In service, I remember watching her more than anyone else on the platform. I saw the Lord in her. I remember she wore an all-white dress—very godly and modest.

"Her singing was powerful! Whether the tempo was slow or fast, it was all powerful! In ministering, she moved about the platform and altar. I don't remember her standing behind the pulpit for long periods of time. I didn't know the word 'anointed' back then, but the emotional and spiritual feelings I remember experiencing—I can say, she was indeed anointed!

"I recall the sense that Sister Willie really loved people. There was no reluctance on her part to reach out and minister to people.

"Though powerful in her ministry, she was not boisterous or loud. She was gentle, humble and meek. I wish I could remember points she made in her messages, but I do not. I did not yet know the Lord, but I remember a feeling of warmth and happiness when she preached. I remember the good response of the congregation around me.

"After I was saved in my teen years, my elders told me of miracles and people being saved in her revivals. When I was older, I learned about Sister Willie's family background, her homelife, and her marriage. What heartbreaking personal obstacles she had to overcome.

"Every ministry that draws souls and shakes hell has a high price tag. Sister Willie paid the price and was willing to sacrifice all for the work of the Lord. There are some chosen and anointed vessels called and sent by God who are one of a kind and will never be duplicated or replaced. Sister Willie was one such vessel."

David Fauss, pastor of Bethel Tabernacle in Houston, Texas, shared many fond memories of Sister Willie. "She frequently came to our church when I was growing up," said Fauss. "I don't know how Dad ever got associated with her, but she and Sister Charlene came by several times for revivals, and it was always a great blessing.

"She had a powerful impact on our church. She wore a cape most of the time and would swing that cape around as she was preaching and walking the aisles. She was all over the church when she preached. When I picture her, it's not in the pulpit, it's in the aisles of the old church, and I can just see her waving that cape. She would grab one side of it and kind of twirl around a little bit, and it was just such a unique ministry and very powerful.

"As a young person, I was terrified she was going to stop and say something to me. She would frequently be used in the gifts of the Spirit and pray for people in the pew. God would reveal things to her. I don't know what I had done that I was worried about, but I felt like I was in the presence of a prophet or an angel.

"This was at the tail end of the Latter Rain Movement. My grandfather had been quite a stabilizing force during the Latter Rain Movement which made him leery of the gifts of the Spirit somewhat because they'd been so abused.[119] Looking back on it, for her to be accepted and used in the powerful way she was, it was just amazing and everybody loved her.

"She packed the place out when we'd have her come. A lot of people wanted to hear her. She told some of the things about her life, but most of it I didn't find out until later, especially some of the things Brother Daniel Scott revealed to us. That made her an even bigger hero than we realized.

"She was a very powerful woman and had a tremendous effect on me. I was about ten years old, and man, she was tremendously used of the Lord—that's all I can say. It was just an absolute amazing thing to see her operate.

---

119 Oliver Fauss founded the church and eventually served as the General Superintendent of the United Pentecostal Church International.

"Our church is an old church. It's going to be 90 years old this coming year. There were healings and miracles, and the Word she gave was so powerful and encouraging. Of all the people who came to our church (and there were a lot of great ministers), she was a high point.

"To this day, the older saints, if you mention Sister Willie, they all have very positive comments about her. I never heard one negative thing."

This picture ran in many advertisements for revivals, including the *Indianapolis Star*, January 12, 1957, page 10.

Photo used in songbook published in the 1950s.

1958

Twenty-one Seniors receive their diplomas. Giant fire at Midway Tabernacle calls for a new addition and considerable repair.

In spite of the setback caused by the church fire, God blessed ABI during this year. Revival with Rev. Willie Johnson was a time of rededication for all. Every month, the Missions class turned attention to the foreign fields through a special school devotion. Rev. Fred Kinzie preached the graduation message where James McElhaney, president, Charles Kiefling, vice-president and Patti Crowell, secretary-treasurer led their class through the doors of ABI into their ministries.

Back row: Jim McElhaney, Jim Wood, Charles Kiefling, Roger Foxx, Jack Leaman
Middle row: Irvin Warsh, Belle Phillips, Fred Asario, Merlyc Bjorklund
Front row: Pat Crowell, Hilda Laita, Dolly Loeffler, Irma Tlitt, Delores Slater, Joanne Jordin

FIRE: MIDWAY TABERNACLE

58

Apostolic Bible Institute
yearbook, 1987,
historical tribute.

Alright

Alright
Alright
Jesus will fix it alright
Alright
Alright
Jesus will make it alright[120]

120 Author unknown.

Chapter 9

ALRIGHT

Another Open Door

O n May 10, 1957, Sister Willie's husband passed away at Charleston General Hospital. He was 74 years old, and his cause of death was chronic asthmatic bronchitis and emphysema.[121] Daniel Scott had known Sister Willie since 1947, but he became her pastor in the years of her ministry as a widow, and during those years she confided in him much of the heartbreak she had suffered. The pastoral connection, however, was only part of their relationship.

"I had grown up under Willie's ministry," said Scott. "She came to our church, Chesapeake Apostolic, to preach revivals. One day I came to church. I'd been preaching for quite some time, but I came with sort of a vest on, and I had on a yellow shirt over it that hung out. I had the cuffs turned up and she came running to me. We were already close friends at that time, but I was just a member in the church.

"She said, 'Son, if you're going to be in the ministry, you're going to have to dress like one.' I never wore that again."

Daniel Scott said he "inherited Willie" when he and his wife Joy assumed the pastorship of the Open Door Church after Bud Entsminger's passing. Scott and his wife had been evangelizing, and

---

121 Based on his death certificate per Linda Brown (nurse).

in May, 1957, through a series of revival services at Open Door, the church doubled. "We had an outstanding meeting," said Scott, "People were slain in the Spirit. Brother Entsminger was baptizing people as fast as we could bring them through to the Holy Ghost in the altar."

In a conversation between Bud and Goldie Entsminger following the special services, the pastor said to his wife, "The people fell in love with the Scotts. If anything happens to me, I want that boy to pastor my church."

Bud Entsminger had founded the church and sacrificed greatly for it. He had also established the House of Mercy Home for the sick elderly in 1949 and had a mission that worked out of the church. There were bunks and supplies in the basement where he would bring people in who needed help.

After Brother Entsminger passed on Easter Sunday of 1958, his wife called Daniel Scott, but Scott had already accepted a position in Philadelphia and felt he was in the will of God to take it. Goldie, however, would not be lightly dismissed. She called again and said, "Brother Scott, can't you come to this church?"

"Sister Entsminger, I can't. I've got things already lined up."

Goldie called again a half a dozen times. She was desperate. She didn't know what to do, so she asked if Scott would come help the church find a pastor. Scott cancelled the revivals he had scheduled and traveled to Charleston in September of 1958 to help the Open Door Church find a pastor. All this happened just four months after Sister Willie's husband died.

"I brought my friends that were excellent ministers," said Scott. "They were already experienced pastors, and there were twelve preachers on the platform that had come out from under Brother Entsminger's ministry. Each one of them thought he should have been the heir, but that was not the church's mind."

In February, after five months of searching, Daniel Scott told Goldie Entsminger, "We're going to have to get this settled somehow. I've got to fulfill what I feel is right, and I promised I would be in Philadelphia."

At the following Sunday night service, Goldie, who was dearly loved by the people, stood and spoke to the congregation, "I need to say something."

She turned to the platform, fanned out her hand, and said, "Why are we searching for a pastor? Our David is already here."

This frustrated Scott, although he kept his emotions in check and did not speak his mind. After the service, six young men asked Scott if he would go out to lunch with them. The group included Eugene and Jimmy Ramsey, the sons of the frontrunner of the church.

After they had eaten, one of the men said, "Brother Scott, we had this planned to ask you to pray about being our pastor. You have brought such peace to our church and our congregation. You've honored Brother Entsminger so much that our church would prosper and flourish under your ministry, and we're asking you to at least pray about it."

Up until that moment Scott had refused to even talk about the possibility. That night he went home frustrated, but God gave him a dream as he slept.

"In the dream God revealed to me that the Open Door Church had lost its first love," said Scott. "I had plans to start a church in the 'city of love,' but the 'city of love' God had for me was the Open Door."

Daniel Scott explained his feelings after the dream this way, "It was a voice from God in a dream that I remember to this moment, and yet I could not accept the dream. I was promised to Pennsylvania. I had committed myself to the district. Everything had been approved. I didn't know what to do."

With God's voice echoing in his spirit, Scott called his presbyter who said, "Brother Danny, the church is probably far beyond your experience. I would strongly recommend that you not go there."

Scott questioned him further, "What should I do? I'm here ministering, the church is responding, and I had this dream?"

Scott offered a suggestion to his presbyter. "Let's have a meeting, and if 100 percent (which is completely out of any logic with those men who want the church themselves)—if 100 percent vote for me, I'll take it."

The presbyter thought it was a waste of time, but Scott said, "Either do it for me, or I'm leaving."

That's how Daniel Scott, a young 24–25 year old man, became Willie Johnson's pastor.

Memories from Daniel Scott

"The first revival meeting we had with Sister Willie was in January of 1959," said Scott. "I had only been pastor less than a year. I asked her to come, and she consented.

"Oh, man, we had a revival. It was powerful. It was absolutely wonderful.

"Over time I started calling her Mama Willie, and I, as her pastor, asked her to hold the first Sunday after New Year every year for the beginning of revival services. She consented because she loved the people, too, and she would stay for two to five weeks of revival services. That's how we became so close.

"She didn't call me Brother Scott, she called me Son. From that moment, I was Son and she was Mama Willie.

"In the winter, my wife and I would pick her up for church and take her home because she wouldn't drive in the snow or in icy conditions. She lived in Slip Hill, five or six miles from the church in Charleston."

Although Scott was unsure of Sister Willie's residence when the Johnson's first moved from Moundsville to the Charleston area, he vividly remembered the white house with the brilliant "Santa Claus Red" steps and shutters in Slip Hill.

"You couldn't miss it," said Scott with a smile. "In front of the house was a set of 15 to 20 steps you had to use to go up to her house. She loved red and white."

The house was somewhat elongated and went into the depth of the hill. The Scotts would drive up into the driveway and go in the back door. When bringing her home from a service, Scott recalled, "Nothing would do her but us to come in. There was no way to deny an invitation to share a time of fellowship in her kitchen. Sometimes we had hot chocolate, sometimes coffee—a cookie or a cake."

Daniel Scott's wife, Joy, recalled a time Sister Willie invited the couple to her home, "She called us one time and told us to come out. Charlene was there and so was an elderly lady that used to travel with her. Charlene had made chili, and we all ate chili, and that chili was chili.

"She said, 'Oh, it's good for you. It won't hurt you.'

"I was a little leery about eating it, it being so hot. And bless my heart, I got sick that night and somebody else did, too."

"She poured herself out in ministry," said Daniel Scott, "She would preach for forty minutes to an hour, but time meant nothing.

"In my mind I can see this as though it was last night. I would introduce her, and Ruthie Collins (my organist) would play the whole time. Ruthie was excellent, and she would catch Willie's spirit. I don't know if Willie mentioned anything to her or not, but Ruthie was playing softly, and when Willie stood up with her cape on, she took the four or five steps to the pulpit and started singing,

In shady green pastures so rich and so sweet,
God leads his dear children along.

"Her eyes would just cloud over. She was completely lost in the ministry of the song—

Where the water's cool flow bathes the weary one's feet,
God leads His dear children along.

"She would sling that cape—

Some through the water, some through the flood,
Some through the fire, but all through the blood;
Some through great sorrow, but God gives a song,
In the night season and all the day long.

"I can never remember a time that the congregation was so great. The church was so full, and the building had been made of second-hand materials. I was scared the trusses underneath would give way, but in that congregation, people came from everywhere.

"The church was crowded like that in every one of her revivals. When Willie would sing like that, the tears would flow and a Spirit cloaked the congregation. She touched people's hearts.

"Willie was at home in the Spirit. When she would throw that cape back, it was not theatrically—it was a ministry making a demonstration that even though you go through the valleys of despair, you've got a God who is able to resolve your problem. By the time she would finish that song, her ministry was already doing the work it needed to do.

"She urged me lots of times about love. There were times I'm sure I was a little harsh on the congregation, and she would sort of mildly rebuke me for it. She said, 'They're sheep. You're their shepherd.'

"She molded my ministry that way, and I got to the point (from that time under Willie's ministry) that I grew up ministering to the hurting.

"I ministered to her many times about her husband. She would tell me. She was broken over it. She couldn't tell it all in the pulpit, but when we got to her home, she would talk about sleeping on the glider. She slept one night with her back propped against the door because he locked her out, and she 'quoted' the Scripture, 'The foxes have holes and the birds of the air have nests, but I have nowhere to lay my head.'[122]

"Our church had a rail on both sides of the altar. We had large drapes that came down, and Willie would come and cross over the pulpit still talking—no microphone—just preaching. She would walk down on the main floor, go back in the congregation, single out somebody that might be in the middle of the pew, make her way in there, pray for that person and never miss a word. Then back to the pulpit she would go. That was her ministry.

"Many times she would play the piano when she sang. Ruthie would be on the organ. She would get to a part in the song, get up, go minister to somebody, go back to the piano and hit it at the same note she left.

---

122 Luke 9:58.

"Willie was lost in ministry. She had absolutely no motive but to get to that grieving or abused heart—to that brokenness—to that backslider. She intended to make a difference. That was my Willie, my Mama Willie."

When God called Daniel Scott from the Open Door Church in 1968, Scott said, "He called me with an audible voice to be a missionary to Ecuador. I wept. I didn't want to be contrary to God's will, but to leave that church—it hurts even yet today. Those people were so precious. Willie was a part of that."

Doug Rashall, who had been a member and served as assistant pastor of the Open Door during Scott's tenure, pastored for a brief season after the Scotts left in 1969. In 1971, however, Billy Joe (B. J.) Sowards took over the position and pastored until his death.

B. J.'s son, Chris Sowards, said, "Sister Willie was part of Open Door Church when we came. Open Door was her church." He remembered Sister Willie traveling and also that "she lived in absolute poverty. Mom and Dad made sure they watched out for her and provided for her."

Sister Willie lived on Hampshire Drive in Charleston next to Woodlawn Elementary School. As a child, Randy Witt would look for her when he was out on the playground.

"After her husband passed," said Witt, "I was honored to assist my father, Clifford Witt, in repairing her washing machine. I was honored to pick up some groceries for her. She lived a very humble lifestyle."

Witt provided a current picture of Sister Willie's house in Slip Hill, but the building bears only a vague resemblance to how it appeared in Sister Willie's day.

"The house was always painted white when she was living there as best as I can remember," said Witt. "It was always neat around it.

Current picture of Sister Willie's house in Slip Hill
(Charleston area). Photo by Randy Witt.

"The section of the house with the lower roof across the front was originally the front porch. It had a half-wall type of banister around it. There was a center entrance to it about where the 'V' is on the house today. That's where the steps went up to the porch.

"Just think of the great men and women of God that have been on that porch—Billy Cole, Shirley Cole, J. C. Cole, Mary Cole, Daniel Scott, Joretta Scott, and a host of others! Wow! If those floorboards could talk."

All Day Long I've
Been with Jesus

All day long I've been with Jesus
It has been a glorious day
I have stepped up one step higher on this glorious King's highway
I have spoken words of kindness
Jesus knows if I've done wrong
I will go and make it right so I can testify tonight
I've been with Jesus all day long [123]

---

123 African Folk Hymn.

Chapter 10

ALL DAY LONG I'VE BEEN WITH JESUS

Prayer and Preparation

Sister Willie did not have any formal training for preaching,[124] but Joy Scott, who knew Sister Willie since her childhood, believes her strongest spiritual attributes were prayer and fasting. Joy's husband Daniel agreed, "She centered her ministry a lot about prayer. She was a woman of prayer. She mentioned many times, 'Son, you cannot minister to people unless you're in touch with the One who can solve the problems.'"

It was said, "In prayer, Willie Johnson empties herself of all, and waits upon God to fill her with His Spirit and mind. Before she will minister, she demands much the same of a congregation. She will not minister until the atmosphere is right."[125]

Ella May Stark was Sister Willie's friend for four decades. She said she saw Sister Willie "lie on her bed and moan for the mind of God. Between services, she never shopped or went out. She'd stay in her room and pray."[126]

---

124 Per Delores Ramsey.
125 Per *Pioneer Pentecostal Women*.
126 Ibid.

Sister Willie stayed in many different homes. Her preparations to minister varied according to her environment, the needs of the congregations, and her relationship with the people she was with, but her spiritual disciplines were attested to by all who knew her.

David White said, "She would come down for breakfast and eat, and then she would go back to her room and probably be there until 3:00 or 4:00 p.m. Then after, she would come down and have supper.

"I think she was a lot like my grandfather. After I would go to bed, I would hear them pray. My grandfather, I heard him pray all night. You could hear her in her bedroom praying sometimes in the wee hours of the morning.

"She never took a note that I know of. She had her Bible, her Scripture. Sometimes she would read it, and sometimes she wouldn't. She was a firm believer, 'You open your mouth; the Lord will fill it.'"

Sister Willie often ministered in Huntington, West Virginia. LaVona Sauters remembered her ministry there. "One thing I loved about the Huntington people," said Sauters, "you would go into their homes, and even in the daytime, they would be down on their knees having prayer.

"Going past people's houses, you would hear them praying, go in, find a chair, and kneel down, too, and pray. By the time the prayer was finished, it might be five or six ladies in there.

"It was just the same way with Sister Willie. If she come by your house, she'd be in there praying with you. They weren't entertained by radio or television. They were entertained by the presence of God. I'm sure when she went by a saint's house, she went in and prayed with them."

While Sister Willie may have lacked formal training, her ministry proved she was an avid student of the Word of God.[127] She knew the Word and would quote Scripture.[128] Her Bible was all marked up.[129] "To me," said Randy Witt, "she had a deep understanding of the Word, how to pray in faith, and operate at the unction of the Holy Ghost."

---

127 Per Neva Limones and Kenneth Mendenhall.
128 Per LaVona Sauters.
129 Per Daniel Scott.

While well-versed in the Word, Sister Willie did not give exegetical messages or offer didactic teaching. Allen Donham recalled Sister Willie being invited to preach in W. T. Poling's church. This pastor's approach to ministry was completely different from Sister Willie's.

"Brother Poling would get in the Bible, get in the Word," said Donham. "He was a good teacher, and he would preach well, and he was respected, and God blessed his ministry. Sister Willie was just different. She was going to sing and say some things, and tears will flow, and everyone else will start crying, too. And there will be a nice move of God.

"Brother Poling always sat behind Sister Willie on the platform and would continually whisper, *'Give them the Word. Give them the Word.'*

"He wanted doctrine, Acts 2:38 right down the line. Nothing wrong with it, but it was just a cute thing—*'Give them the Word. Give them the Word.'*

"A bunch of people would get the Holy Ghost and healed, and everyone left happy and joyful and full of the Spirit. So Brother Poling was happy with the end result, but his method of getting that result differed a little bit. She taught us from the University of Hard Knocks, and about 'kneeology,' tears, and being broken."

Chris Sowards agreed that Sister Willie's ministry wasn't Bible expository teaching, but he added, "I never heard her minister that she didn't open up with a Scripture. And I heard her many times (usually after having someone in the building read the verses), she would comment a little about each verse, and then say, 'Now they can't say I didn't preach any Word.'"

Sowards believed Sister Willie's ministry changed people's lives where they lived. He said, "She was masterful at getting down on their level and giving them hope that they could change."

Bob Gilstrap noted that when Sister Willie stayed in his home she did not spend the whole day in her room. "She prayed, studied, but she also was there for the meals and would visit with us. She didn't isolate herself, yet she liked to sleep late (being up late at night and ministering). I think she was very normal in her pattern of praying, fasting, and study."

She did not, however, engage with people before service, added Gilstrap. "We lived in the parsonage right next door. She would come over at normal time for service, and after would linger awhile. She didn't race out like some . . . but she didn't come early and visit. Her rapport with the people was just normal."

James Stark, on the other hand, said, "She would come down and eat with the family, but she stayed in her room most of the time. We would not see her until late.

"I never remember her coming to breakfast. I don't remember if Grandma would take anything to her. Charlene would sometimes come down and take things to her. She pretty much stayed in her room except one meal a day."

After services at Open Door, Daniel Scott said Sister Willie would want to leave church right away.[130] "She didn't want to have to answer a lot of questions," said Scott, "She wanted her pulpit ministry to answer the questions. I would usher her out the back door. I can't remember staying around any time. I would take her home."

---

130 Also told by Allen Donham.

My Thanks to Him

Verse 1

I love to tell how Jesus saved my soul
When I was lost and facing dark despair
But mortal tongue could never tell the whole
Nor thank Him for such wondrous love and care

Refrain

He is more than all the world to me
The dearest friend that I have ever known
And it will take the whole eternity
To thank Him for the love that He has shown

Verse 2

When I am sad He brings me hope and cheer
He gives me grace when-e'er the way is rough
How could I thank Him for such blessings here
My life on earth will not be long enough

Verse 3

Tho' I should live a thousand years below
And praise the Lord from dawn till set of sun
Still that would not be time enough to show
My thanks to Him for all that He has done[131]

---

131 Words and music by A. L. Clanton. Published in "Memories and Modern Songs," Edited by John T. Cook, published by Stamps Quartet Music Company, Dallas, Texas, 1955.

Chapter 11

MY THANKS
TO HIM

The 1960s

Sister Willie and Charlene Day continued their ministry throughout the 1960s. Don Martin recalled her coming to Cisco, Texas, in 1960 to Pastor Fronie Blackwell's church. "I remember loving her style of music and the cape she wore," said Martin.

**OLD FASHION
REVIVAL**
CONTINUES
HEAR
Sister **WILLIE JOHNSON**
Preach and Sing The Gospel in a
most UNUSUAL WAY ! !

EACH NIGHT AT 7:45 EXCEPT MONDAY
EVERYONE WELCOME TO
PEACE TABERNACLE
5th St. & Ave. U
John Kershaw—Pastor
A UNITED PENTECOSTAL CHURCH

*Lubbock Avalanche-Journal,
July 2, 1960, Saturday, page 7.*

In the early 1960s, Sister Willie preached for Fred Foster. His son Tom shared his memories:

"She would dress all in white with that tam hat she wore, black cape, white lining. And she could evermore preach and just move everybody. I've seen grown men just run to the altar.

"I was just a kid when she'd come once a year. We moved to Houston when Dad started Texas Bible College in '63, so it had to be 1959 to 1963. What a preacher—a woman.

"We would travel. I remember going with my mom, my brothers, and sister, and we would go other places where she was preaching.

"She was a power preacher. She preached Holy Ghost revival and was very emotional. She'd throw that head back and she'd sing. She'd preach. She'd sing. Sister Charlene would travel with her. She'd play the organ (dududududuh). They worked together as a team.

"If I remember, one of Sister Willie's records, the vinyl (which was normally black) was red.

"Crowds would come and move. People would shout, dance, and get the Holy Ghost. I was a kid—and I got the Holy Ghost in 1960—so I'd be just right in there shouting with them, praising God. I was a little feller.

"She'd just get up and was herself—wild, loud, but she was very feminine."

Kenneth Mendenhall recalled Sister Willie ministering at the opening of Texas Bible College, "They asked her to come and sing, and she said, 'You've came here not acting like you're acting today—so formal—and all these officials here.' She got loud and started singing, and there was a move of the Spirit."

Sim Strickland, who also heard Sister Willie at Texas Bible College, remembered Sister Willie powerfully singing "Shut in With God" as she walked the aisles of the sanctuary. "Oh, how I remember," he reminisced.

Kenneth and Bobbye Wendell attended Texas Bible College for two years before their missionary appointment to Ethiopia in 1968. The couple knew their call, but they had not made it public. Sister Wendell shared details of their confirmation.

"It was a long time ago," said Bobbye Wendell. "We were married in '49, got the Holy Ghost in '59, and we went to the Bible school in January, 1965. Looking back on it, Sister Willie Johnson being at that school was good timing for us—for me.

"When we went down, it was for my husband to go to Bible school. I was going to work. Brother Fred Foster, the president, called me in and mentioned that if we were both called to the mission field, I really needed to be in school also. So I did enroll, and I drove a school bus nine routes a day part of the time. I kept books on the side for small businesses that just wanted somebody to post things up for them, and I worked for an export trading company. We had four children of our own and one relative we were taking care of at the time.

"My husband and I were the oldest full-time students. We weren't old (in our 30s), but not that many married people were going to school full time. We were so hungry and thirsty for teaching, and we had the cream of the crop.

"When we first arrived at the school, Sister Willie was holding revival at Brother Kilgore's and she would come. She didn't know me from anybody. I was just one of the students in chapel service.

"When she started in that day, it just touched my heart all the way to the bottom. I don't remember what all she said, but my heart was so full. I was standing and worshiping and weeping. She put her hands on me, prayed for me and said, 'You have the call. You have the burden.'

"There was something that happened that day. I didn't need anyone to tell me I had a call, but when someone like her came and confirmed it, that offered a lot of strength to someone who was just so new to that realm of service. Right after that, we announced publicly we were called to Ethiopia. It was done right there at the Bible school chapel.

"Sister Willie was such a forceful, dynamic person, and yet so clothed in humility. It wasn't a great big ministry. I heard her many times after that when we were traveling and would be in Oklahoma and different places. As far as building a sermon, it wasn't that type of ministry. She was just 'people to people'—she ministered to people, and there was such an impact."

"She preached a revival in Muncie, Indiana, in 1960 for Brother Dick Martin," recalled Martyn Ballestero. "Our family based out of that church while my dad evangelized. We were there for a year. My sister, Beverly, who was fourteen months younger than I, received the Holy Ghost during that revival.

"Sister Willie preached with the black cape around her shoulders. She would twist around with a flair. I have memories of her playing the piano and singing, and no preaching because people would come to the altar and get the Holy Ghost. It seems like she was there for about a month. I have fond memories of her."

Sister Willie preached several revivals for Donald Haymon, founding pastor, at Calvary Apostolic Church in Denver, Colorado. "I can visualize her even now," said Haymon. "With the cape waving royally behind her, she dashes down and around the aisles proclaiming the good news that Jesus Christ is Lord!"

Haymon added that the last of several revivals she preached for him was in 1963. "Always productive," said Haymon, "this final revival with this dear lady resulted in 15-year-old Samuel Stewart Kelly receiving the Holy Ghost. He lay on his back, speaking in the tongues of angels far past dismissal time." Sam became Haymon's brother-in-law and served the church forty years as "orchestra director, sound engineer, and all-around faithful servant of the Lord."

"I was a very young teenager or younger when she ministered in Parkersburg, West Virginia, in the late 1960s," said Michell Cole, who was impressed with Sister Willie's ability to understand the moving of the Spirit and meet the needs of the people. "I was greatly in awe of her," she shared. "I know my pastor, J. C. Cole, loved having her in our church, and my mother loved it when she came. We never missed a service when she was there."

Of the ministry in Parkersburg, a report was made in the *West Virginia District News*:

We have been especially blessed in Parkersburg in having Evangelist Willie Johnson with us. During this revival, thirty were baptized in the name of Jesus and quite a number received the Holy Ghost. Some nights, we could not seat the large crowds and the good revival spirit is continuing.

"She came to Revival Tabernacle and held a revival. In fact, she came there twice, I think, and Sister Charlene was assisting her in playing the piano.

"She more or less sang her messages. I loved her singing. She's the only one that I know of that I could sit and listen to until 11:00 or 12:00 at night. She was fascinating, and she would just keep you inspired.

"She was at our church in San Diego, and it was a rough time our pastor was going through. His daughter had run off with somebody. Sister Willie gave the type of message that he needed, and I guess the rest of the church needed it, too."

—George Adams

"I have wonderful memories of Sis. Willie Johnson when she would hold services in Claremore, Oklahoma, at the United Pentecostal Church pastored by Rev. C. A. Nelson. I was a teenager or in my early twenties when I heard her. I loved to hear her preach and sing, accompanied by Sister Charlene on the organ.

"I felt the way she preached she was sent to encourage the church. That she did! I believe that at times the Lord would give her a word of knowledge about someone as she walked around and through the congregation preaching. I never heard her call anyone out, but she had a way of making a statement and pausing at the end of your pew, making direct eye contact with you, and then moving on.

"Her songs were very moving and anointed as well. I'll
never forget her singing with the Texas Bible College Choir
at the Oklahoma Campground! They brought the house down
with one called, 'Jesus!' I wish I had one of her albums on
CD today."

—Ruby Bickford

"My son, Mark, was three years old, and Sister Willie was
his most favorite person in the world. I couldn't keep him
away from her. One morning late in 1962, Sister Willie
Johnson was in the Appleton, Wisconsin, church praying.
Mark had been told not to bother her when she was praying.

"When Mark found her, she was laying face down by
the altar praying. Mark quietly squatted beside her head
and softly said, 'What's the matter, Brother Willie? You fall
down? Let me pray for you, Brother Willie.'

"Then he put both hands on her head and loudly said,
'Rise up and walk in Jesuses names, Brother Willie.'

"She loved telling that experience."

—Joe Holland

Another boyhood memory came from James Stark:

"My grandfather received the Holy Ghost in the church in
Bridgeport when Sister Willie was preaching a revival, so she was a
part of our family for years.

"When I was probably eight, I swallowed a ball bearing. My dad
had given me the ball out of a large ball bearing about the size of
marble. It was steel. It was so smooth, and I put it in my mouth and
swallowed it.[132]

"Sister Willie came the next week. The doctor had told my mother
that if I didn't pass the ball, they would have to do surgery and take it

---

132 James Stark noted that his wife Christine found the x-ray in their basement the week of
his first interview for the writing of this book.

out. My mom told Sister Willie, and after dinner one night she pulled me up on her lap in Grandpa and Grandma's dining room, and she began to pray for me. Within two days I passed the ball bearing.

"I remember a time she said she would be with us for a one-week meeting. Our little church was between the railroad tracks and the beer joint, and the house was built against the church. There was a feed store across the street.

"You couldn't have found a place to park a car, so they sent me out to wait for Sister Willie. She'd gotten a hotel someplace and was driving in to start service.

"She and Charlene got there about half an hour after church started in a big, blue Cadillac. I remember when it turned the corner and started up the street toward the church. Charlene was driving and Sister Willie rolled the window down (power windows—and that was a big deal in those days). She rolled it down and they found a place to park and got out and came in. Having her in the house was an amazing experience."

Dan Scott, pastor of Christ Church Nashville, and son of Sister Willie's pastor, Daniel Scott, shared an experience from his younger years:

"I knew Sister Willie Johnson as a child. My grandmother knew her, and she was close to our family. She was the most remarkable person. She had a wisdom and grounding that was just extraordinary. She had spiritual gifts, and she also had charismatic presence. She knew how to perform, but it wasn't manipulative. There was something behind it. She wasn't just selling a sizzle without a steak. She was humble of heart.

"When I was working on my master's degree for mental health work, we were put on the spot one day to quickly tell how a non-psychologist had (in our minds) shifted our life's trajectory in a significant way toward psychological health. I hadn't thought of it in years, but it came to me with such force and emotion, so I told the story.

"As I was going through puberty, about twelve years old, I was convinced I must have demons. I wasn't in an oppressive church, but we didn't get much sexual education in those days. I waited until she was in town one night, and after church I told her I wanted to talk to her.

"She sat on the pew with me with rapt attention, just like I was the only person in the world. 'I thought you might cast out my demons,' I said.

"'Oh, my,' she answered, 'That's a serious thing.' She asked me what I had been experiencing.

"'I think about naked people.'

"'Sometimes, or pretty much all of the time?' she asked. I was ashamed and looked at the ground.

"Sister Willie said, 'I'm going to pray for you now.' And she prayed, 'Lord, thank You for making this a normal boy in every way and preparing him to be a good man, a righteous man—and that You always teach us to control the forces in our lives, and he will grow up to be an upright person.' Then she kissed me on the forehead, and I was just dazed.

"I just wonder what it would be like in our times. Some people are just not that well-grounded in life—the damage they could have caused. I'm immensely grateful for not only her wonderful charismatic gifts, but for her wisdom."

From 1966 to 1968, Larry Neal served as assistant to Richard Martin, who pastored Parkview Apostolic Church in Muncie, Indiana. "It was in '67," said Neal, "Brother Martin wanted her to come for revival, but she didn't want to come and stay. She wanted to come nightly from Indianapolis because she was at her son Scottie's house. Charlene was there, too. So Brother Martin sent me to get them. I got them, and they stayed awhile, and they went back. Then they drove up once.

"They came up and got bad weather—real icy and snowy. They left, and they said they would be going back to Indianapolis. Everybody said, 'Be careful!' They didn't much more than get a few blocks away and they got cold feet. They got a room at the hotel, and she didn't tell anybody until it was all over.

"At the closing of that revival, I talked to Sister Willie. I said, 'Sister Willie, you don't know what you're doing for us—us young preachers. You don't know how much you mean to us.' She said, 'Yes, I do. I sure do.'"

Karen Harding was five years old when she received the Holy Ghost at a revival Sister Willie was holding at Parkview Apostolic. "Sister Willie would sing a lot, and it was marvelous!" said Harding. "We had all her records. I remember two songs the most, 'God Leads Us Along' and 'I Trust in God.' I still sing both songs to this day!

"I remember thinking as a child, *I want to do this when I grow up!* She made me want to minister and sing!

"It wasn't until I was a teenager that I heard of her woes. She was married to a sinner man. From what I heard, he drank a lot. After she got saved and started preaching and singing in churches, her husband did not like it. Many times he locked her out of the house and would take her little love offerings from the churches and buy rounds of drinks for the men at the bars.

"She just kept preaching and singing. There was just something about her. I watched one time as she walked the aisles singing 'Love Lifted Me.' She took the hand of a sinner man while she was singing, and he crumpled to the floor under the power of God! It was something else.

"Also, I remember her cape—black velvet with a white satin lining. (Wish I had one.) She would lift her arm and wave that cape very dramatically! Many times, sections of people would fall out or tremble under the power of God when she waved that cape in their section of the church! Powerful! She was highly anointed!

"I thank God for the gift of Evangelist Willie Johnson! I'm doing what I do because of her influence on my young life!"[133]

Margaret Mitchell was the first lady of Parkview Apostolic Church of Muncie,[134] and served alongside her husband, Richard. "Willie Johnson was a very outstanding person," said Margaret. "Her ministry was unbelievable. She held mighty, mighty revivals, and she sure had the mind of God."

---

133 Karen Harding recorded "God Leads Us Along" on her "My Heritage, Vol. 1" project.
134 Richard Martin passed in 2014, and the church previously known as Parkview changed names to River of Life and is now pastored by Richard Martin's son, John Martin.

When preaching at Parkview, Sister Willie stayed in the Martin's home where she filled the house with piano music, singing, and prayer. "It was singing and worship and church all the time," said Margaret. "She was just full of it. All she did was pray. She was so dedicated to the work of God. That lady had power. Our altars were flooded after she would preach.

"We had lots of funny things happen. She was a lot of fun—a down-to-earth, good person who just made everybody feel good. We ended up calling her Grandma Willie."

Diana Snider was six or seven years old when Sister Willie visited the church she attended in Claremore, Oklahoma. "She would always come in late and proceed down the aisle with the big, white cape on," said Snider. "When she began to sing, the Spirit would begin to fall.

"I don't remember any of her messages, but I remember her presence. When she walked in, you just knew she was a woman of God. I don't remember any other preacher from that time in my life some 55 years ago, but she made a believer out of me that women could minister in word and song."

"James Stewart, the former pastor of the church I pastor in Columbus and former District Superintendent of the Ohio District, came from the church in Jewett," said James Stark. "He was raised on a little farm just outside there. His family was Methodist—probably the premier family in the Methodist church in Jewett.

"When my Uncle Hugh witnessed to his friend Jim and brought him to church and he got baptized and got the Holy Ghost; it caused a horrible rift in the community of about one thousand people. Jim's mother, Evelyn, loved our Bible studies. She would come every Thursday night to hear my grandfather's Bible study. She and my mother were good friends. She came to hear Sister Willie at my mother's request, and she left before Mother could get to her. She showed up the next Thursday for Bible study and had no idea the revival was still going on.

"She came into my grandparent's house where there was no central heating. We had heat upstairs only from the registers in the floor. Sister Willie always had the room over the dining room. Consequently, because of that arrangement, you could hear everything said in the dining room up in her room.

"Evelyn came in before church and just laid into my mother about how much she didn't like that woman that was there the week before. Sister Willie was upstairs, and my mother was dying a thousand deaths because her friend had nothing nice to say about her.

"After Evelyn said her piece, she went on over to church. Mother never did tell her Sister Willie was still there. Church started and Sister Willie came down and went through the house. Usually she went in the side door of the church in the front up by the altar on the right-hand side, and she would just go through the backyard instead of the front door.

"Evelyn was in the church and had no idea revival was still going on when Sister Willie walked in that front door. It wouldn't have been polite to walk out, but she wanted to.

"Sister Willie got up and started to preach. She walked back down the aisle and walked over to Evelyn and put her arms around her. She received the Holy Ghost right there in Sister Willie's arms."

Donna McGray's mother was the Evelyn in the above encounter. She recalled Sister Willie's visits, as well.

"She came here when I was in my teens," said Donna. "My mother and Ella May Stark were very good friends. Before we came into the church, my mother was telling her, 'I just don't believe in women preachers at all.'

"I remember her coming the first time after we got in the church when I was probably seven years old. I had never been in that kind of church. We were Methodist, and I was not used to that activity in church.

"I remember her coming down the aisles and she always wore this cape—and really, at first it scared me. I'd never seen anything like that before, but after she came, we just fell in love with her."

REVIVAL TIME

Beginning Sun., Jan. 31
7:30 P.M. Each Evening

WITH EVANGELIST

Willie Johnson

with us again

Parkview Apostolic Church

1010 E. Centennial—Across from McCulloch Park

*We Still Believe in an Old-Fashioned Holy Ghost,
God Sent Revival! Come and See!*

Revival at Parkview Apostolic, *Muncie Evening Press*,
January 30, 1960, Saturday, page 5.

According to Rick Stoops, his mother, Edith, had been going through the darkest trial of her life before Sister Willie came to town. "She went to church, and Sister Willie Johnson was preaching that night," said Stoops. "Sister Johnson suddenly stopped, pointed to Mother, and said, 'Sister, don't you know God loves you?'

"Instantly, God touched Mom, and her great trial was over as God brought peace and the joy of the Holy Ghost in a wave of glory."

Alice Torres met Sister Willie when she was holding a revival in California in the 1960s. Sister Willie and Charlene stayed in her home for a few days while a place was readied for them in the church. Alice was a young mother and there were three children in the house.

"I think she needed her own space to pray," she said, but she was pleased the women were able to use her children's bunk beds in their accommodations at the church.

"She kind of took me under her wing while she was there," said Alice. "I got to do her laundry and take care of little needs she and Charlene had."

The revival lasted six weeks, and Alice could not remember if they took even one night off to rest. After the series of meetings, Alice and her friend followed Sister Willie to Oakland on their nights off as she ministered there for four weeks.

"She really didn't have to preach," said Alice. "She just had to sing, but she did preach and she would walk among the crowd and touch people, and the Lord would move. All she had to do was walk into a room, and the Holy Ghost fell. Being close to her was like walking with the Lord.

"I love her so much. I still sing her songs. I cannot tell you how she helped my walk with God. She knelt beside me and prayed. I had a long road to go along."

Neva Limones, the daughter of Sister Willie's pastor, Daniel Scott, had many memories to share:

"She was a beautiful lady—inside and out—and was such a sweet woman, kind and caring," said Neva. "And when she preached, God would show her ways to minister to people. It was awesome to see! It would make one tremble in the presence of God.

"I heard her tell of how she was going to end her life and was walking to the river when she felt compelled to stop in a church. That's when God worked in her life and she dedicated herself to Him.

"Throughout my life, her music and songs have helped me and given me strength. I just love to put on a CD and sing along with it.

"We went to visit her once in the wintertime. I was ten or eleven years old. Her house was a nice little cottage on the side of the mountain. It had a bright red door and there were many steps leading up to it, which were also painted red.

"There was quite a bit of snow on the ground. My parents drove up the driveway and went to the door, but Sister Willie's daughter told us she had gone to the store at the foot of the hill. My brother and sister and I stayed outside and played in the snow.

"She saw us up on the hill from where she was down at a store. In a while, Sister Willie drove up and got out of the car, dragging a brand new sled with bright red runners behind her. She laughed and said it was for us. She had seen us playing while she was at the store and wanted us to have a good time while she visited with our parents."

In 1960, the Strickland family moved to San Pablo, California. "I don't remember the first year she and Sister Day came there," said Jerry Strickland, "but she came several times before we moved back to Arkansas in 1968.

"What a lady of God. I will never forget her walking across the front, preaching, and wearing that black cape. My mother bought all the records, and most of the specials my mom sang were Sister Willie's songs."

Edwin Harper grew up in Morgantown and later pastored the Morgantown church. "I knew Willie all my life," said Harper. "She was bigger than life in our part of the world.

"Until I began to pastor, she was a star figure on a platform singing and preaching. In my years at Morgantown (I began pastoring as a 25-year-old man), she stayed in our home. I was so grateful we were able to have contact with her.

"Once Sister Willie spent time in our home, and she told my children, 'It's nice to come in and go to the bed and not look to the floor and see the chickens underneath the house.'"

On a different occasion, the Harper family took Sister Willie to Lakeview Country Club for a meal. There was a huge buffet spread out. "When we walked in," said Harper, "she said, 'Oh, my God, my God. So much food—so little me.'"

"She was quite given to the gifts of the Spirit," related Harper. He recalled a time in particular two women who were relatives had been "having a competitive fuss." He said, "It was to the point they said, 'If you're going there, I'm not going there.'"

Sister Willie was in the area ministering in a church on the west side of Huntington. Neither of the quarreling women knew the other was going to the service, and when they arrived, they sat on opposite sides of the church.

"Willie was ministering," said Harper. "She comes down the aisle with her famed cape flying. She stopped and looked at one side and said, 'Young lady, stand up.' Then she pointed at the other lady and said, 'You, too.'

"She began to tell them what was going on and told the women God was mad at them and they needed to go to the front, make peace, and repent. She was that gifted in the Holy Ghost."

Another incident occurred in the church Harper pastored. A man from the area who had been a minister in Florida "violated his marriage vows while pastoring" and returned to Morgantown to attend a funeral.

"He was in a service one night, and he always dressed to the nines," said Harper. "He was real, real arrogant—liked to dress up.

"Sister Willie ministered, and he got under conviction. He came to the altar.

"She said, 'Brother Harper, could I have some oil?'

"She took a big bottle and poured the whole thing on his head—the whole enchilada was on his head and spilled out on his lavender sport coat.

"She took her hands and massaged that oil in his head, and he fell out speaking in tongues on his back. That was part of her mode of operandi. She was something else."

Revival at Open Door, 1960s.

Douglas Rashall was at the Open Door in 1965 when Daniel Scott pastored, and when Scott left for missions work in Ecuador in 1969, he became pastor and stayed until 1971.

"I knew of her before then," said Rashall. "She used to evangelize in the Houston area where I was from, though I never went to hear her.

"Every January she preached a revival. It was just a tradition that had been going on for years, and we kept it going. She would come home for Christmas, and before she left, she would preach a revival for us. Charlene was traveling with her at that time. She just played the organ.

"As far as messages, her ministry was just singing and zeroing in on people she saw conviction on. I actually heard her take a text and preach a typical message just one time. Most of the time it was singing and walking and she worked the crowd. She could spot a backslider when they walked in the door and she zeroed in on them.

"She came across real well. The people in Charleston just loved her. It would almost have been an uproar if I hadn't had her for revival every January.

"I remember she had no telephone at her home (and of course it was before cell phones), and almost invariably sometime in January she'd get sick and you didn't know it until she didn't show up at church. So you had to be ready to preach if she didn't show up. More than once."

Brenda Cobbler grew up in Charleston and was a member of Open Door in the '60s and '70s. "Many people throughout my adult life have had debates over whether they believe women should be preachers," said Cobbler. "All that still comes to my mind each time I hear the debates is the powerful preaching of this woman of God! I know without a doubt she was not only a woman of God, but an anointed and powerful minister of the gospel! I loved it when she held revival."

The first time Buddy Barnett heard Sister Willie preach was in 1968. "I was home on leave from the Navy and was about to be shipped to Vietnam in just a few weeks. My grandparents attended Faith Temple in Baytown, Texas, and invited me and my girlfriend to attend a service (which was really not something I had planned to do in the short time I had before I had to go back to duties aboard ship).

"Sister Willie Johnson was the visiting evangelist the night we went. She did not speak for very long before it seemed she was looking right into my soul. Before she closed her message, I found myself fighting back tears of conviction.

"I had my girlfriend with me, and I didn't know how she would react if I yielded to what I was feeling. Then Sister Willie left the platform and walked down the aisle to the end of the pew where we were sitting. She looked me right in the eye and said, 'How about it, Sailor?'[135]

"I clutched the wood bench with both hands so hard my knuckles turned white, but I did not go to the altar that night. It was several years later after I returned to civilian life and found the Lord that I encountered Sister Willie Johnson again.

---

135 He was in uniform.

"I ended up pastoring a little church in Mont Belvieu, Texas, and had Sister Willie preach several times. We became good friends. I will always remember her as one of the sweetest and most sincere followers of the Lord I have ever known."

Sister Willie influenced Charlie Ganey's ministry "in more ways than one, especially her way of ministry and music." Ganey expressed his thankfulness for having met her in Baytown, Texas, in 1968.

Sharri Ballard also remembered Sister Willie's influence on her Christian faith. "She was an absolute treasure," she said, "just the joy and excitement she would bring to our church when she visited us was so contagious."

"She was a mighty warrior in the kingdom of God in the '60s and '70s," said Dorothy Nalley. "I was privileged to hear her many times at Open Door in Charleston. Just thinking about her made me pull out a tape I have of her singing 'His Eye is on the Sparrow.'"

Revival, *The Odessa American*, February 12, 1961, Sunday, page 6.

Ronald Brian giving Sister Willie a fish he caught, Glendale, Arizona, 1969.

Sister Willie with Doris Hosch,
Dallas, Texas, May, 1967.

SISTER WILLIE JOHNSON

Sister Willie's photo used in "I Trust
in God" album promotion.

In her preaching uniform
in later years.

Outside
church
holding
a plate of
goodies.

Ministering in Texas, 1966,
picture provided by Elizabeth Lopez.

I'd Be Willing, Lord, to Run All the Way

Verse 1
Use me, Lord, in Thy service
Draw me nearer every day
I will be willing, Lord, to run all the way
If I falter while I'm trying
Don't be angry, let me stay
I'll be willing, Lord, to run all the way

Verse 2
Pained by heart aches, scorned by loved ones
A little sunshine now and then
There are mountains in my life so hard to climb.
But I promise I'll keep climbing
If You'll only let me stand
I will be willing to run all the way

Verse 3
When I've done my last ... service
and there's nothing more that I can do
just a weary tired pilgrim, sad and alone
Only linger ever near me
While I near my home, sweet home
I will be willing to run all the way[136]

136 Author unknown.

Chapter 12

I'D BE WILLING, LORD, TO RUN ALL THE WAY

Willie Johnson's Unique Ministry

Sister Willie's ministry could not be pigeon-holed into one neat category. She was a gifted singer, communicator, and minister. The following presents some of the hallmarks of her service to the body of Christ.

EVANGELISTIC MINISTRY

"Willie was the ultimate evangelist; such a godly woman."
— Kenneth Mendenhall

"She touched people with the love of God. That was the hallmark of her ministry to me. I just see her as a very powerful woman who was in the Holy Ghost. It was an exciting thing. When I look back over my growing up years, of all the evangelists that came, definitely she was a high point.

"She gave people a lot of hope and faith. I think she knew what people were going through, and she touched on it and strengthened the church. From my viewpoint now (after being in the ministry for almost fifty years), I look back on it and I would have her right now in a heartbeat.

"She ministered from the heart, and she listened to God to tell her what to say and point out who she needed to talk to. She wasn't concerned about having a perfect sermon. She was more about reaching souls."

—David Fauss

George Adams, along with many others, mentioned he had seen some of the best preachers, but Sister Willie was "just one of the most outstanding evangelists I've ever known."

PROPHETIC MINISTRY

"Sister Johnson, was our beloved hero here in West Virginia. She lived not far from where I live, in a humble home. Her influence was far and wide. Our former beloved Bishop Billy Cole noted her to be one of the truest God-called prophetesses he ever had the privilege of knowing."

—Jarrod Price

"She was a prophet of God. She prayed for my dad. He had an ear removed because of cancer and was supposed to get radiation treatments, but didn't. He lived for 30 more years!"

—Wanda West

"She could read you like a book. My daddy was a backslider, and she went to him one night and said, 'Morris, you need to get up to that altar and give your life back to God. You're too good of a man to go to hell.' And he did. He served the Lord until he died.

"She could read you and knew what you needed to hear. She would go out in the audience and pray for the people that

needed to be prayed for. Her ministry was just very strong
and very personal to people."

—LaVona Sauters

"She was 'spot on' with me," said Roger Zimmerman. "She didn't
know me at all. Nobody else knew what I was dealing with and the
anger I had built up inside of me, but God revealed it to her, and she
just nailed me right to the seat."

"She could read people's spirits. She prophesied over me a
number of times, and without exception, they've all come
true. I learned to expect it."

—Daniel Scott

"Robert Mitchell passed a couple of years ago. I remember
he flew to West Virginia to see her. He said he had come
with two questions. When he arrived at her house, there
she was sitting on the porch, and before he got there, she
answered them.

"She was absolutely operating in the Spirit. God would
speak to her, and the way she would minister, she would help
people, no matter who they were."

—Chris Sowards

Edwin Harper of Morgantown had never personally met Sister
Willie when she first prophesied over him. Three times in his life she
came to him and spoke the same words God had given him directly as
he sought Him in prayer. She prophesied his call to the ministry.

Not only was Sister Willie prophetically gifted, James Stark
recalled, "She preached more from the prophets than probably anybody
I ever heard. She wore Jeremiah out." Daniel Scott also remembered
her preaching regularly from Isaiah 43:1–3:

*But now thus saith the L*ORD *that created thee, O Jacob, and he that formed thee, O Israel, Fear not: for I have redeemed thee, I have called thee by thy name; thou art mine.*

When thou passest through the waters, I will be with thee; and through the rivers, they shall not overflow thee: when thou walkest through the fire, thou shalt not be burned; neither shall the flame kindle upon thee.

*For I am the L*ORD *thy God, the Holy One of Israel, thy Saviour: I gave Egypt for thy ransom, Ethiopia and Seba for thee.*

"She consistently dwelled on the phrase, 'I am the Lord thy God,'" said Scott.

DISCREET AND KIND

"Sister Willie walked through the sanctuary, put the mic down, and whispered in people's ears. Then she would walk off and no one knew what she had said. Later, the people in the congregation would tell me she told them just what they had been doing.

"She wore a big cape and terrified me when I was little. She walked up and down the aisles and operated in the Spirit in the gifts, but she did it in a way that was kind."

—Chris Sowards

"When you would go to her services, you knew you wanted to make things right with God, because God told her things. She would not embarrass anyone, but she would discreetly talk to you if it was very personal."

—Linda McGinnis

"She never shamed anyone or forced them by putting them on the spot, but she spoke honestly, and with conviction, caring for the souls."

—Neva Limones

AN AVANT-GARDE WOMAN

"She was absolutely before her time in the anointing and gifting that she operated in."

—Andrew Fowler

"This lady had tapped into what you could read about in the Bible, but I had never really seen until she came into my life, even though I had grown up in church."

—Roger Zimmerman

"She was a prophet in every sense of the word, and I think she was really before her time."

—Chris Sowards

CONFIDENT

Sister Willie ministered for decades in the church David White's grandfather founded. "She took free reign when she was here," said White. "If she felt led to do something, she didn't ask permission. She just did it."

Although Sister Willie often spoke gently, Neva Limones said her ministry was "firm and bold with the power of God behind it. She could have whispered, and it would have such impact. It was the Holy Spirit and not her forcefulness in any way.

"I never remember her raising her voice too much. No screeching—she was a lady in every sense of the word."

Neva also recalled a story she heard from her parents told to them by Sister Willie. "One minister didn't like long preaching," recalled Neva, "so before church, he set the hands on the clock ahead, so it would look later than it actually was. The Lord revealed this to Sister Willie, and she called him out for it. It was said he had a nervous breakdown, but he later apologized for it, and the Lord healed him."

HANDS-ON

Sister Willie's ministry was hands-on. She touched people when she prayed for them, men and women alike.

"As she was going down the aisle she would lay hands on people, and the power of God would get those people."
—David White

"She yielded to the Holy Ghost perfectly and was a willing vessel."
—Allen Donham

Bob Gilstrap remembered her personal style of ministry as she moved about the church touching people. "Especially the first few rows," said Gilstrap. "She would stop and lay her hands on somebody, then it became just her and that lady or man.

"'You're in trouble, aren't you?' she'd say. 'You need a touch right now, don't you?' Then she would pray. It was powerful."

COMFORTING AND COMPASSIONATE

"Her ministry was to the hurting. That was her entire ministry. Broken homes were healed through her ministry— and broken hearts. God would lead her to go to people during the service and minister to them."
—Daniel Scott

"Sister Willie showed God's grace and strength to her audience."
—Allen Donham

ANIMATED

Sister Willie moved and was loud at times, "but but she didn't jump and shout," said Lavona Sauters. "People listened to her intently."

Doug Rashall recalled Sister Willie singing "God Leads Us Along," one of her most popular songs. "When she sang that," said Rashall, "she was moving through the crowd swinging that cape she had and rolling her eyes at people zeroing in on them. She was quite a character."

"She moved around the congregation," said Neva Limones. "It seemed that the altar area was the whole church. You would never hear her screaming or hardly raising her voice, but you trembled when she walked by!"

A WORSHIPPER

"She liked to sing and then preach in between, and then she'd sing a little bit more and then preach a little bit more. Then she'd sing—then she'd express something—a little story about what was going on."

—Teresa Schanzer

"I can hear her in my head! She talked of the Word and she ministered, sometimes bursting out in song."

—Neva Limones

A STORYTELLER

"Sister Willie held people's attention not because she was a great preacher," said David White, "but she was a storyteller. She would walk the aisles and tell stories and emphasize different things.

"She was her own lady. It was never cookie cutter. She didn't pull punches. She would just lay it out as it was. She told stories about Scott, the kids, places she'd been and the things that had happened. She would weave that into a sermon.

"Sometimes she wouldn't even take a text. She would just 'remember when . . .' and talk about how God moved in this situation and that situation. It would spark faith in people. There were deliverances, healing, people being saved because of that style of preaching."

Roger Zimmerman compared Sister Willie's storytelling to parables. "They were stories of a lot of her life, but she also was able to relate those stories on the level where anybody could understand and relate to them and be drawn. She would take the audience and have them in the palm of her hand in just a matter of minutes. She could work a crowd."

"Willie rarely opened her Bible on the pulpit," said Daniel Scott. "She quoted the Scriptures she wanted to speak from and went into ministry immediately. No elaborating. She would quote about going through the fire and water and then minister. She used herself as examples and stories of abusiveness would come in."

Bob Gilstrap evangelized fourteen years, pastored forty, and taught one year at Texas Bible College. In his evaluation of Sister Willie's ministry, he said, "Sister Johnson had her style that was totally different from anyone we ever had. I don't see that style of ministry now. Instead of sermonizing, Sister Willie would take a text, talk about the woman at the well or whatever, but then walk through the audience. She would minister, sing, then come down off the platform and minister to the crowd in such a beautiful way."

Allen Donham also believed Sister Willie's forte was telling stories and provided some additional thoughts. "They were probably very true stories," recounted Donham. "There was always something spiritual and sometimes funny, but she did not always complete her stories. She would tell the story of somebody—maybe Uncle Charlie who got up in a tree out on a branch that's just about ready to break. Then she goes on to something else, and people are shouting, but at the end of the service they are wondering what happened to Uncle Charlie."[137]

INTENTIONAL

James Stark said Sister Willie always had a theme song for revivals. "The last revival she preached for us in Jewett, she used the chorus of 'Blessed Assurance,'" said Stark. "She didn't do much with the verses. She would preach a little bit and sing,

This is my story, this is my song.

"Maybe that's all she'd get out. She'd stop and preach a little bit longer, but that was the song she used.

"My memory says she was probably never any more dramatic than she was in that meeting. She knew the people loved her, and she would tell things about her life and then break into,

This is my story, this is my song, praising my Savior all the day long.

"She sang that chorus every service of that meeting. If she stayed someplace very long, her meetings were almost like a series. She wouldn't preach the same thing, but the theme for the meeting would be the same. It was like she would tap into a vein of the Holy Ghost of what the people in the church needed at that time, and she would get a song and just hit the same thing."

MIRACULOUS

In addition to the testimonies of miracles that happened throughout Sister Willie's ministry recorded in previous chapters, Barbara Gilstrap

---

137 James Stark mentioned Sister Willie's stories weren't always complete or finished. Her object was to make a point and get a response.

added her personal experience. Early in the 1960s, Barbara went to church with an infection in her body.

"I went up to be prayed for," she said, "and the moment Sister Willie touched my head, I started to dance. I fell out. I couldn't have held myself up at all, and I was totally healed."

Sister Willie ministered regularly to physical needs. Opal Wittington was attending a service in Charleston when B. J. Sowards was serving as pastor. The woman had suffered a back injury and was in constant, severe pain. Without prior knowledge, Sister Willie discerned Opal's situation, walked down the aisle, and placed her hand right on the injured spot. As she touched Opal's back, she was instantly healed.[138]

Daniel Scott recalled many times Sister Willie ministered in their annual New Year's revival services. "She would pick out different individuals in the congregation and go to them," said Scott, "and without hesitation or introduction, she would pray and that person would be healed."[139] Scott recalled how God gave her discernment to call out in prayer the exact conditions when so many times there was no way she could have known by observation only.

A lady named Cindy said, "I remember Sister Willie Johnson. She was holding a revival at our church in Dallas. When she laid hands on me and prayed for me, I was healed of epilepsy."

"My mother stood about 5'6" or 7" and weighed less than one hundred pounds," said David White. "She was really, really thin. She'd had some nervous problems.

"Sister Willie was at the house, and she said, 'Betty Jean, I'm going to pray the Lord will put some meat on your bones.' She came back,

---

138 Retold from an account recorded in *Pioneer Pentecostal Women.*
139 Quote from *Pioneer Pentecostal Women.*

and Mom had gone from 90 to 165 pounds. She came in and saw her and said, 'My God, I'm going to tell the Lord to quit!'"

"She prayed for my grandfather, Jack Myers, in Miami, and he was immediately delivered from nicotine. He told me years later (when I was a boy) that a terrible taste came up out of his mouth when she prayed for him, and he never had a desire for a cigarette again."

—David Meyers

EFFECTIVE

"If she could not get you to the altar when she was preaching a revival, nobody was going to be able to," said Jimmy Ramsey. "She could get you under conviction."

"Her ministry was all about hope and restoration," said Linda McGinnis, "and not playing games with God."

"She would preach and people would get under so much conviction," said Martha Ann Martin. "She had a way about her to reach people and help them make the choice. Very compelling ministry."

Bob Gilstrap said, "When I was a kid in the 'Willie era,' we would have an altar call and everyone would come and kneel and pray and we would have glorious times."

Daniel Scott recalled altar services when Sister Willie ministered. "Service erupted," said Scott. "They just came to the altar. Altar service 'just happened.'"

Scott went on to say, "Everybody loved her. I never heard any bad thing about her, ever. People responded so favorably. She could talk to most of the people she knew from Charleston and tell them exactly what they needed to do, and they listened."

"People submitted to her ministry," said Neva Limones. "They accepted her ministry as the Word of God. Even though we feared (in a good way), we still wanted to hear it. We considered it a privilege and honor to have her there."

Randy Witt said that in his church, everyone got behind Sister Willie and responded to her. "She was greatly loved and respected! People had no doubt that she walked in the Holy Ghost and operated in the gifts of the Spirit!"

"Her life and ministry transformed our lives and ministry," said Allen Donham, "and we're just so very grateful to have known her."

EMPOWERING/INSPIRING

Sister Willie didn't let people wallow in self-pity. Neither would she let them criticize God for their crosses. She believed trials proved a person's love for God, and cross-bearing was a common topic throughout her ministry.[140]

In fact, Sister Willie would often pinch herself and say, "I still live in this, and this flesh still gives Sister Willie trouble! We're not divine yet! Some saints are precious, precious, precious saints. You can't say that about all saints, 'cause some saints ain't precious!"[141]

Sister Willie prodded believers to mature in their faith.
"This is not just Holy Ghost, not just tongues. He's got nine beautiful gifts for you, but you gotta grow up!"[142]

She charged the people to stand out from the crowd and worship God as His peculiar people.

---

140 Per *Pioneer Pentecostal Women.*
141 Quote from *Pioneer Pentecostal Women.*
142 Ibid.

"How many of you are peculiar? If we don't act peculiar and different—hair pins flying out of your hair and all that little tuff you got in there fall out on the ground—and act peculiar, ain't nobody gonna listen to us."[143]

She rallied the congregation.
"Saints, He's called us for a purpose. We have His work to do. Don't ever let go of your ministry!"[144]

She inspired the struggling.
"You know, temptation is a part of life, but with the temptation, my God makes a way of escape. If you want to escape, don't try to avoid the temptation; face it, overcome it, grow in God by overcoming!"[145]

She roused people to higher faith.
"Don't be ashamed to ask for more God. You ain't never gonna get all the Holy Ghost you can get. Keep getting you some more! There's a height, a depth, a dimension you can swim in. . . . Leap out by faith!"[146]

She stirred the static soul.
"Holy Spirit, thou art welcome in this place" (she wept as she spoke the words and repeatedly thumped her fists against her chest) "—this place."[147]

Bob Gilstrap summarized the inspirational effects of Sister Willie's ministry on his life:

---

143 Ibid.
144 Ibid.
145 Ibid.
146 Ibid.
147 Ibid.

"She impressed me, challenged me. In fact, she still does—to be a minister instead of a preacher. . . . It's alright to have a good, organized sermon with notes, but a minister is there because of the needs of the audience.

"She's long gone, but she still challenges me to try to minister to people and to help them. She was in tune with the Lord—an uplifter.

"Sister Willie faced the problems of life with 'God's going to help us; He's going to lift us up, encourage us, strengthen us.' When that happens, people get healed."

Sister Willie preached in some of the United Pentecostal Church International's largest congregations for decades[148] Among the places she ministered were Life Tabernacle of Houston, Texas, under James Kilgore; Calvary Apostolic Tabernacle of Bellflower, California, under Sam White; Christian Life Church and College in Stockton, California, under Clyde and Kenneth Haney; Calvary Tabernacle in Indianapolis, Indiana, under Nathaniel Urshan; Texas Bible College; Apostolic Bible Institute in Minnesota, and many more.

James Stark offered some background on Sister Willie's first connection with Apostolic Bible Institute (ABI). "Richard Davis, who had pastored in Portsmouth, Ohio, and then gone to ABI and was pastoring in Eau Claire, Wisconsin, brought her to his church for a revival," said Stark. "He had graduated from ABI and was pastoring in Eau Claire, which was not a horribly long way from St. Paul. Brother S. G. Norris would not have her at St. Paul, but the students started slipping away from St. Paul to go to Eau Claire when they could get away. So finally, after so many of the students were coming back talking about the meeting, Brother Norris had her come to ABI and hold service in the old Midway Tabernacle."

The meeting was held in the mid-1950s. At this time, Sister Jessie Norris, wife of Pastor S. G. Norris, had been teaching ABI students

---

148 Confirmed by Crystal A. Napier, archivist at the Center for the Study of Oneness Pentecostalism.

the necessity of giving everything to the work of God. As Sister Willie ministered, Jessie Norris told the students, "Now you watch, that's the way to hold a revival."[149]

Sister Willie continued to travel and minister and draw big crowds. Sanctuaries filled to overcapacity. "She drew a crowd," said Roger Zimmerman. "I'm in the eastern panhandle of West Virginia. Whenever she was around, people would travel an hour to an hour-and-a-half to get to a service where she was at back in the early '70s."

"She just automatically drew people," said David White. "It was good. She was one of the few who believed in the 'body ministry.' It wasn't just the preachers and elders, but the body of Christ laid hands on people and prayed and ministered to people."

Dreama Malik remembered Sister Willie's revivals at the 25th Street Pentecostal Church. "My mom started into church there by herself when she was fourteen," said Malik. "She married at sixteen to my Daddy from Ohio. My Dad used to go hear Sister Willie preach as a young teenager. My brother and I would travel to Huntington, West Virginia, to visit my grandparents and go to 25th Street Pentecostal Church to hear Sister Willie Johnson preach. Some of the most powerful services I have ever been in. Such anointing. Chairs lined the center aisle. People standing along the walls and standing room only in the back of the church. I was just a teenager then."

149 A representative from Apostolic Bible Institute confirmed S. G. Norris would regularly have guest ministers in the first couple of months of the year, and revivals were usually held around the same time. Quote from Pioneer Pentecostal Women.

I Cannot Fail the Lord

I cannot fail the Lord
I cannot fail the Lord
He has never failed me yet
Every problem He has met
And I cannot fail the Lord[150]

---

150 Attributed to Doris Akers. No copyright information found.

Chapter 13

I CANNOT FAIL THE LORD

The 1970s

The 1970s brought continued ministry opportunities for Sister Willie. Roxanna Place attended revivals Sister Willie preached at Calvary Tabernacle in Three Oaks, Michigan, and remembered the songs she sang, "Sweet Holy Spirit" and "God Leads Us Along."

Sandee Huffman and her husband rented their first home from Sister Willie when they were newlyweds, and her father did bodywork on Sister Willie's last car, including painting it candy apple red. Sandee said she loved the huge smile on Sister Willie's face when she first saw the car.

"We shared many meals with her," said Sandee, "and loved when she preached at the Open Door. She would tell my pastor, B. J. Sowards, 'Keep them crying, Pastor. There's strength in humbleness and tears.'"

Sandee considered Sister Willie a great mentor and example. "You don't forget people like that," she said. "Because of her, I know you can obtain higher places with God here on earth that only comes through visiting God's throne room every day."

In 1971, B. J. Sowards and his wife were elected pastor of Open Door church. In 1979, the church purchased property on Kanawha

Boulevard—the Gray Stone Motel. It was an old motel with 32 rooms, but they saw it as an Apostolic church, and it would come to play an important part in Sister Willie's future.

Chris Sowards remembered Sister Willie's ministry at the Open Door in the 1970s, "I've never met anyone like her—powerful lady— and kind. She just had a way about her. I've seen her just look toward big, old, strong guys, and they would weep and run to the altar."

Sowards also recalled some humorous moments. "She talked about Fasteeth (a denture adhesive). I remember one night in the old church she was preaching and her teeth fell out. She said, 'Raise your hands and praise the Lord.' Then she looked at my brother-in-law and said, 'Pick them up.'

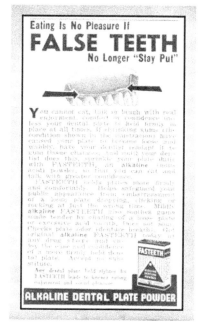

Fasteeth ad.

"He looked at her and picked them up. She put them back in, spun around in her big cape, and started preaching again.

"I remember once when church was over, someone was there with a new baby. She spun around and asked, 'Whose baby is that?'

"People questioned her, 'What's wrong?'

"'That baby's going to be a real problem,' she responded.

"The people were kind of offended, but boy, that came to pass. She was out of the pulpit, but still operated in the prophetic everywhere she was. She was one you wanted to always be clean. You didn't want her to look you in the eye if you had any sin in your life. But I never saw her abusive to anybody.

"She was funny. She would tell the funniest stories—real-life stories about people getting angry, mad, making eyes at someone else's husband, music going, sing a song—fast, then slow. I've never seen anybody ever like her. I've seen people try to be like her, but she was unique in every sense of the word."

Sowards admired her music ability—her singing. "I was blessed," he said. "I played music, and I remember her coming to get me." In the Sowards's remodeling efforts of the motel they had purchased for their church, the pastor and his wife made an apartment for Sister Willie at the church. "She had her own room that was for her anytime she wanted it," said Sowards. "I was probably sixteen then, and I remember her taking me down to the sanctuary and she would sit down beside me on the piano. She taught me how to play minors and black keys. I would hit a note and she'd say, 'Not it. Not it.' Then, 'There you go.'"

E. C. Sowards was B. J.'s brother, and he pastored in Huntington, West Virginia. His daughter, Carolyn, recalled Sister Willie's ministry in her father's church. "She preached a six-week revival that brought in many of the saints that were there until my dad retired."

Easter with Becky Collins Fowler at Open Door Church in Charleston, WV.

Billy Cole, Albert Kelbaugh,
and Willie Johnson (L-R).

Sister Willie later years.

Debbie Kitchen worked for Brother and Sister E. C. Sowards in the '70s. She said Sister Willie held revivals and preached for Brother Sowards many times, and she always stayed in the Sowards's home in an upstairs room when she ministered in Huntington.

"Services were held Sunday through Friday," said Kitchen, "and she would always sing before preaching. She loved 'His Eye is on the Sparrow' and would sing it before most of her messages."

Sister Willie spent a lot of time in prayer. Kitchen recalled hearing her pray for hours while she cleaned and cooked in the Sowards's home. She also studied the Word continuously.

"One time when I went upstairs to check on her," said Kitchen, "she had several Bibles and commentaries around her with her reading glasses low on her nose diligently reading, studying, and researching for hours."

One day, while Debbie Kitchen cleaned, her friend Connie (who had recently been released from rehab and filled with the Holy Ghost) came to visit. Connie talked of how she had not been able to give up cigarettes and felt helpless not knowing how or what to do. Sister Willie, who was downstairs at the time, walked over to her and said, "Let's just pray."

Sister Willie fell on her knees, took the young woman's hands, and began to weep and pray in the Spirit. The presence of the Lord filled the room, and after five or six minutes, Connie began to cough.

Kitchen was concerned she might be choking, but Sister Willie kept praying. Suddenly Connie coughed, and a black glob came out. "God immediately delivered her from cigarettes," said Kitchen, "and she has never had another from that moment until this day, over forty-plus years later."

Another day, as Kitchen worked upstairs, Sister Willie called to her, "Child, come in here." When Kitchen joined her in the room, she told the girl, "My husband was a mean man, but without Scott Johnson, there would have never been a Willie Johnson."

Sister Willie went on to tell Kitchen about a night she had gone to church with her daughter, Gloria. When they arrived back home, they were locked out. Sister Willie said she took off her coat, wrapped her baby in it, and slept in a swing all night. The next morning Scott unlocked the door, and Sister Willie went inside.

"I love you. I want to be obedient to you," said Sister Willie to Scott, "but I have to be obedient to God and serve Him."

Kitchen recalled a time Sister Willie accepted an invitation to preach a revival in northern West Virginia. The church sent her a train ticket, but she had no money for food or a berth on the two-day trip.

She thought perhaps the Lord wanted her to fast. When she boarded the train, she was already hungry. She headed to the dining car to see if she could get some water.

She sat up all night, and the next morning she suffered a crick in her neck. Sister Willie told Kitchen, "I was so hungry I could hear the growling and mauling of hunger to my backbone."

The next morning the starved woman had to endure the aroma of fresh-baked rolls, coffee (she loved coffee), and other foods. She thought, "Lord, this is a hard fast!"

After Sister Willie arrived at her destination, she was picked up and taken to the church. When she walked in, they had prepared a banquet for her. There was pork roast, pot roast, meatloaf, potatoes, and coffee. "All kinds of wonderful foods and so much of it," said Sister Willie. Kitchen recalled Sister Willie saying she never appreciated a meal more than the feast they prepared, and they had a "Burning Down Revival."

Once during a six-week revival, "Sister Willie called all the children to the front," said Kitchen. "She had them line up and prayed for each child. One child, in particular, she stopped and just stood there looking at him before placing her hand upon his head. She spoke about how God was going to use the child mightily. It was like she could see deep into your soul."

Of her ministry in general, Kitchen said Sister Willie was "mightily used in the gifts of the Spirit, especially the word of knowledge. Whenever Sister Willie was preaching, the church was always packed out, and it was a common occurrence for service to last until 11:00 p.m."

One humorous recollection Kitchen had was of a time Sister Willie was being discharged from the hospital. She had been admitted for pneumonia, and when it was time to leave, Debbie, Connie, and Gloria went to pick her up.

"Did you bring my turban?" Sister Willie asked Gloria.

"No, ma'am!" answered Gloria.

Sister Willie, unwilling to be seen in public with her hair a mess, took a pair of panties and fashioned a turban on her head. Kitchen helped her pin it on. "Connie and I could barely contain our laughter," said Kitchen.

Sister Willie thought no one would notice, but when they got into the elevator, a very tall doctor stepped in with them. "He was looking down at Sister Willie's head," said Kitchen, "and he almost busted out laughing. The look on his face was so funny!"

In the 1970s, Greene Kitchen served as the District Superintendent of the East Central District/West Virginia District of the United Pentecostal Church.[151] At a district conference held in the Huntington Civic Center, Sister Willie sang "Hold to God's Unchanging Hand" with Helen Cole, Jean Urshan, and Marilyn Gazowski. According to Edwin Harper, there was such an incredible anointing, the women sang the same song for thirty minutes in a phenomenal worship service.

Allen Donham recalled Sister Willie's ministry being very effective in Morgantown, personally and for his family and church. "In 1976," said Donham, "I entered the ministry at about age 33, and that's when she really was able to help us. Being in her sunset years, she was able to come and relax and enjoy herself with us, and we had several revivals. It was a wonderful time. Gave us a real jumpstart.

"She was so genuine—just marvelous. A real Holy Ghost-filled, tongue-talking, crying, shouting woman who could preach to 20 or 2,000. It was a glorious experience for us to know her and very impacting."

In 1976, Sister Willie was preaching and singing when Jeneen Angeles received the Holy Ghost. "I was ten years old," said Angeles. "She was singing the song 'Surely the Presence of the Lord is in this Place.' I am now going on fifty-two. Still serving the Lord!"

"She was so anointed when she preached," said Linda Williams, who heard her minister in Wheeling, West Virginia. "You were either laughing or crying, and when she would swing her cape, you knew she was going to preach something that would touch your heart!"

Robin Laird was a teenager in the 1970s when she traveled with her mom and granny from Adena, Ohio, to Wheeling to be in service with Sister Willie. She recalled being terribly afraid of her. "I was told she

---

151 Greene Kitchen was the great-uncle of Debbie Kitchen's husband, Robert L. Kitchen, Jr.

could read your mind!" said Laird. "I was afraid that something bad was in my mind and she would know. . . . Such a memory!"

Kenneth Mendenhall was going through a severe problem at the church he pastored on Indiana Avenue. As he was out driving, he came up to an intersection. "I looked out my window (in the day before you had electric windows)," said Mendenhall, "and I saw an old, beat-up green Cadillac, and Willie was in there. I blew the horn and rolled down the window, but the light changed.

"'I'll see you at the next stoplight,' I called out the window.

"We went to the next light, and she said, 'Brother Mendenhall, God told me something. That whatever you're doing, you're doing right.'

"I was in the midst of a church split, and she didn't know a thing about it. She had discernment.

"She got people to the altar that were in sin. She was preaching at the small church in Morningside in her black shoes, white full dress, and black cape. Somebody had waxed the floor on the platform. It was wooden pine.

"She started to stop, and she couldn't stop.

"She started sliding across the floor, and so we took care of that the next service. That didn't bother her. She laughed about everything."

Betty Goss remembered Sister Willie's music, "I will never forget Sister Willie singing, 'I'm in Love with Jesus, and He's in Love With Me' the many times she spent with our church family at 25th Street Pentecostal Church with our sweet pastor, E. C. Sowards and his sweet wife and mother of our church family playing the organ for Sister Willie. I hold those years spent learning to love God and love each other near and dear to my heart, and it causes me to hold fast to the old pathways. That's where my foundation was formed, and my anchor still holds. Praise God!"

Elizabeth Joy Lopez remembered Sister Willie preaching when she was about six years old. "I thought, 'Well, I've got to take her some money,'" said Lopez, "so I did a little lemonade stand outside. I think we were on the outskirts of Dallas, but I remember my mom put a little lemonade stand for me out there on the sidewalk.

"That little money I made, I took it to Sister Johnson. She was standing at the back of the church and I took it to her.

"I said, 'This is for you if you need it.'

"She said, 'Thank you.'

"That was my offering to her, and I got the Holy Ghost in one of those revivals. I was just a little bitty girl. My heart. It was powerful services. I felt beautiful when she was ministering. I was small, but the ministry she had was what grew up within me. I loved Sister Johnson."

"We were appointed as missionaries with the United Pentecostal Church in October of 1974," said Alan Demos. "Our first week of deputation . . . we arrived in Flatwoods, West Virginia, with our small daughter, Laura, and had a service with Pastor Dennison, his wife, and their small daughter. Later that week, we had a service with Brother Howard Saffle at Riverside Apostolic Church in Morgantown, West Virginia.[152]

"In that service, knowing that a missionary to Greece was to be there, came the Rev. Anthony Morfessis, a priest with the Greek Orthodox Church in America.

"He was baptized in the Holy Ghost with the evidence of speaking in other tongues, and, most surprisingly, was baptized by immersion (the Greek method, albeit of infants) in the name of Jesus Christ. The speaker for these meetings which he attended, and when he received the Holy Ghost baptism, was none other than Sister Willie Johnson."

Allen Donham shared more in-depth details of this event.

"Father Anthony Morfessis was a priest," said Donham. "He came to one of her revivals. He would not come in the church—not that he felt himself too good, he felt himself (I think if I can use my

---

152 This church was subsequently pastored by Edwin Harper, and later by David Hudson.

own description and discernment)—he felt uncomfortable. He was a very humble man.

"The platform at Riverside Apostolic had a door on it where people could come up the backstairs and come up to the platform. They would come up from the basement.

"Father Anthony sat at the bottom of the stairs. He wanted to hear Sister Willie. He wanted to know more about the Holy Spirit. While she was preaching to the audience, they left the door open on the platform so he could hear the message. Sister Willie didn't mind at all. She loved that type of thing.

"During the service the Lord really moved, and finally, Sister Willie, with her beautiful way of enticing people into the Spirit and to come to Christ, got Father Anthony to walk up the steps. He came up on the platform, where in due time he received the Holy Ghost.

"The Lord began to use him in the gifts of the Spirit, and he worked in Morgantown for a while in ministry. Then he went to Uniontown. I heard of various miracles that were happening in his ministry and gifts that were working through him.

"It was a marvelous way I believe that God not only reached a soul there, but also used him to reach into Greek Orthodox churches, and people received the Holy Ghost there."[153]

Randy Witt offered a second-hand story from Billy Cole. He said, "As a young man Billy Cole told of Sister Willie coming to hold a revival in Parkersburg, West Virginia, where his father, J. C. Cole pastored. He said Sister Willie was preaching, and about halfway through the message, as she was walking the aisles, she stopped, turned and looked right at him sitting in the congregation. She said,

---

153 At the time of this event, Riverside Apostolic Church was in a year of change. Howard Saffle was retiring, and Edwin Harper was transitioning to pastor. Harper said, "I spent many hours with Father Anthony Morfessis. He received the Holy Ghost while I pastored there." Harper confirmed Willie was the evangelist in the service and added, "Father Anthony became so involved in the Apostolic movement that the hierarchy of the Greek Orthodox Church called him back to Constantinople."

'Billy, you've been fighting again! When I get finished preaching, you'd better hit the altar!' And then kept on preaching.

"Billy said, 'She was right!' He had been fighting."

Billy Cole told on himself in 1991 in a message titled, "Wise Men Still Seek Him," "We miss people like old Sister Willie Johnson. I don't know if you knew her or not. She had so much compassion. And ministered to the people.

"My daddy come from the old school. He liked the Word. I mean he never used a story out of the *Reader's Digest* or never used a story out of the newspaper. If he used a story, it was in the Bible. He was old school, let me tell you.

"Daddy was something else. I remember I was home on furlough one time from Thailand, and we had to go to Charleston to get some cholera shots, and that's where Sister Willie lived. I said to my father, 'Oh, I wish Sister Willie was home. I'd love to see her so much. She had such compassion, and she would minister to people in such a marvelous way, the brokenhearted, you know.'

"And my father said, 'Oh, she just wants to minister to the brokenhearted—minister to the bereaved. I like for someone to take the Word and preach.'

"We were talking like that, and sure enough, Willie was home. She didn't know what you called it, but she had the gift of the word of knowledge and the discerning of spirits—one of the most keenest gifts I've ever seen manifested in anyone.

"So we went up to see her, and she was so glad to see us and embraced us. My dad walked into the living room, and she said, 'Brother Cole, somebody has to minister to the brokenhearted.'

"I'm telling you, she was something else."[154]

---

154 Versions of this story were recounted by many people, including Doug Klinedinst and James Stark.

William Finn remembered Sister Willie from when she held revivals at Harrison Hills United Pentecostal Church in Jewett, Ohio, back in the early '70s. He was just a young boy, but he recalled Sister Willie was "very captivating." He spoke of her as "very real" and of the deep presence of the Lord that accompanied her ministry. "She had an anointing that was very different from other people," said Finn. "She was an amazing woman of God . . . an anointed vessel of God. She was one of a kind.

"She was held in such high esteem, that at the beginning of service, Brother Hugh Rose actually escorted her down the center aisle of the church on his arm and led her to the pulpit. Sister Rose played the organ and he would escort Sister Willie.[155]

"She always wore the cape that had the lining in it and hung down the back, and I remember her singing an old spiritual, 'When the Lord gets ready you've got to move, move, move.'

"She was one of those people that people just loved, respected, and admired. I was just in awe."

Ernest Bass lived in Tulsa, not far from Charlene Day's family. He recalled Sister Willie preaching quite a bit at the First United Pentecostal Church in Tulsa. "One night after church . . . they [Sister Willie and Charlene] decided to go out to eat. Willie always wore that big, old cape. She looked like Batwoman sometimes.

"They were going down our street that we usually go to town on and my wife and I decided we'd go out. We came upon a police car, and outside was Willie, and she was just waving them arms, and that cape was just flying, and she was telling them how she was just a poor preacher. She looked so funny with that cape flying and the police talking to her and the lights.

"She didn't stop at a stop sign, but they didn't give her a ticket. She talked her way out of that one.

---

155 James Stark recalled the same dramatic entrance. "It was in the church in Jewett after my uncle, Hugh Rose, was the pastor (who succeeded my grandfather, Harper Rose)."

"As far as a preacher, she didn't preach great, great, great sermons, but she would sing and Charlene would play, and she'd get to talking about this and talking about that. Before long people were worshipping and praying and crying and coming to the altar. She didn't just preach, she sang and preached, and Charlene played the whole time. That cape a-flying, she was talking and praying. She mostly encouraged so many people.

"We loved her. She was a real fine lady, and Charlene was a real close friend of ours."

"I wanted to play the organ so bad," said Linda McGinnis. "Sister Sowards, the pastor's wife, let me sit on the platform and play my accordion so I could watch what she did with her hands and her feet on the organ."

In 1977, Linda was just twelve years old when Sister Willie prophesied to her, "You will marry a minister and be his organist."[156]

"I did learn to play the organ," said Linda, "and I played for many district functions. I was Billy Cole's organist for a few years. And when Sister Willie came to preach, I said, 'All those years ago when I was trying to play the organ, you prophesied that I would.'

"'And here you are,' she said.

"I did marry a minister, but he failed God and backslid and left me for another woman. That was not God's fault, that was his fault. But everything she said came to pass.

"I've seen her cast out demons. I've seen people delivered of things that just do not happen today. She was very anointed.

"When Sister Willie entered the building, it was pretty dramatic. I remember a time when seemingly no one knew she was coming, but they were very excited she was there. Of course, they asked her to preach.

"As she stepped to the pulpit, I was very impressed with the authority and the spirit she had. I was amazed at how God spoke to her and used her ministry. It was like she just walked with her hand up in the clouds, holding God's hand.

---

156 Linda could not play the organ at that time.

"I would see her many times through my teenage years and very young adulthood, all at Brother Cole's. I would sometimes call up her number, and if she was in town, she would answer, and she would pray for me. She never had to know the whole story of what troubled me. I would just say, 'Sister Willie, it's Linda, and I need prayer,' and she would pray. What a treasure."

Roger Zimmerman first saw Sister Willie when his daughter, Ginger, "was just a strapling of a little girl" and he was in his early 20s. "Her mom had left Ginger and me when Ginger was 15 months old," said Zimmerman, "and I was dealing with all that rejection, hurt, and anger. I had custody of Ginger, but I was so angry I was actually contemplating how to get even with the guy her mother had moved in with.

"Sister Johnson was preaching a revival in Oakland, Maryland, and I was sitting on the second row next to the aisle in the center. She was preaching, and she always wore a black cape. She come off the platform and she whirled that black cape and put her finger on the end of my nose almost and said, 'Thus saith the Lord, *Vengeance is mine, and I will repay.*'

"I just melted in the seat. Just melted.

"The guy was a school bus driver and he picked up the bus at his mom and dad's house. I went there the next morning or shortly thereafter. He came to the door, and I called him by name. I said, 'Look, you know that I was looking for you, but you don't have to worry about that anymore. I'm not going to look for you, or get you in a fight, or anything like that. I tell you one thing, what she did to me, she's going to do to you.' I left, and within a year she did the same thing to him.

"That was my first run-in with Sister Willie Johnson.

"Different times she would have me read for her while she was ministering. She came to the Oakland, Maryland, church on three different occasions. She would call me to the side and put a pencil dot on the Scripture where she wanted me to start or stop. It could be in the middle of a verse or the end. When I look in my Bible, I still see those pencil dots and am reminded of that lady.

"One time she was there—I think it was the last time I saw her—she made a comment while she was preaching, 'I'm just so looking forward to going to heaven. I just hope they have a recliner there, because I'm going to get in that recliner, kick back, and enjoy life.'

"I was still single at the time. I bought a brand new recliner and took it out to the parsonage where she was staying (with the pastor's permission). I took it out the day she was leaving and loaded into the back of her Cadillac and made it waterproof. That was the last time I saw her.

"She made an impact on my life and totally changed my life just with that simple prophetic word she spoke to me on that day. That's a memory that stuck with me and brings tears to my eyes right now just remembering it and talking about it. Ginger was just a little girl—not even two years old then. Had I done what I was contemplating, who knows. You don't know what would have happened. I could have ended up in prison.

"Through all that mess—the divorce and everything—God got my attention and called me into the ministry. I was able to raise Ginger, and she's an ordained minister with the UPC. God has been very, very kind to me.

"I did remarry nine and a half years later, and my son has his general minister's license. He is also the district Youth President. My wife is the district Ladies Ministries President. I have been so blessed, and I owe a big part of it to Willie Johnson and the impact she had on my life."

Ginger added comments of her own about the evangelist who changed her future. "Sister Willie Johnson would come and preach at my home church, Rosedale United Pentecostal Church in Oakland, Maryland. I was young, so I don't remember her messages, per se. What I do remember is her presence and the anointing of God that rested upon her.

"She would come into service with her white cape glowing behind her. She walked in the Holy Ghost. I didn't understand it then, but I do now. It was like Peter in the book of Acts, where the very shadow of him saw the lame and sick healed.

"And when she began to sing in the Spirit, the Holy Ghost would just plumb fall! She preached with fire! She was an old-fashioned Apostolic preacher! She wasn't afraid to preach truth—unadulterated truth!

"You couldn't be in a service with Sister Willie Johnson and *not* be moved. You may leave with the imprint of the pew in front of you emblazoned on your hands, but you did not leave untouched!

"I have one of Sister Willie Johnson's songbooks somewhere in my collection—a treasure! She was one of my heroes as a kid growing up. I . . . will forever remember the cape, the humbleness and the powerful anointing she had!"

"She was always with us in May," said Gracie Mitchell.[157] "She came, and she stayed in my home so I could cook for her and do things for her. We always took her shopping. We bought the white uniforms and bought the black capes, white hose, and white shoes. We would go to stores and look for things she needed. We had a lot of fun. We laughed a lot and cut up.

"We went to see her in Charleston. We visited her in her home and met her sons and daughter. She cooked for us. She cooked cabbage, and we loved it. She cooked it in a different way than we'd ever seen—cooked it whole. It was very good. I don't know how she did it.

"We would go and eat chicken there in Charleston. She would have a place to go always for that.

"She loved to sleep in the morning, but she was spry when she got up. And all afternoon she'd be laughing, talking, and visiting.

"She had a little lady from Three Oaks, Michigan, who traveled with her in the last days. They were very good friends. She would leave her car (an old Cadillac) at her house when she'd travel.

"She was the most gentle, understanding, sympathetic, kind person I ever met. I never met anyone like her. Her anointing—there are no words for it."

---

157 Robert and Gracie Mitchell pastored in Dayton, Ohio. Gracie also recalled her son, Robert, helping Sister Willie put her shoes on her feet.

A story was told by Evangelist Lee Stoneking of a time he was traveling with Billy Cole, Cole's wife Shirley, and Sister Willie. They were driving in West Virginia and pulled into a truck stop to take a break. A truck driver came up to Sister Willie crying and began profusely shaking her hand. The man had been an alcoholic, but he had been delivered at one of her revivals. He said her singing had ministered deeply to him, and in that service, he received his Acts 2:38 experience.[158]

In the mid-1970s Sister Willie travelled with two ladies to the Apostolic Church in Jesus pastored by James Shockey. Kelli Kirchner said the pastor "was not afraid of women preachers. He would give them liberty to preach, and we had a great revival. The church was packed . . . the Holy Ghost fell, and the anointing was there in a mighty way. Sister Johnson sang and preached her heart out. Very fond memories in my teenage years."

---

158 Per Shaun Butler who related the story told by Lee Stoneking in a service.

God is Still on the Throne

Verse 1
When in distress, I call Him
When you're oppressed, just call Him
When you're in doubt and you find no way out
Remember, God is still on the throne

Refrain
God is still on the throne
Within your bosom you have a phone
Where'er ever you walk, you're not walking alone
Remember, God is still on the throne

Verse 2
If all your friends forsake you
The cares of life overtake you
When storms assail you and others have failed you
Remember, God is still on the throne[159]

---

159 Words and music by Roberta Martin, 1959.

Chapter 14

GOD IS STILL
ON THE THRONE

Living Above Prejudice

Prejudice comes in many forms, and Sister Willie Johnson faced her share of unfavorable preconceived opinions ranging on a scale from subtle to overt. Margie Sowards said, "She had persecution plus," but in the same sentence, Sowards gave the key to Sister Willie's strength to overcome—she was a "prayer warrior."

Willie Johnson was black. She was white. She was a woman. She was a woman preacher, and she was Pentecostal.

RACE

Although Sister Willie was a light-skinned woman with an equal amount of African-American blood and Caucasian blood, her race is listed in an official capacity as "negro (black)" on the 1940 census.

Donald Haymon recalled Sister Willie gladly proclaiming, "The whites don't want me; the blacks won't have me, but Jesus's got me!"

Sister Willie's parentage did not deter her from fulfilling her call, even in the early years of her evangelistic ministry. "She was accepted and loved dearly by all," declared Daniel Scott. George Adams agreed, "Even being biracial back in the years ago when some people might not have liked that or had some prejudice about it, there was no prejudice I could see. She was loved by everybody."

Sister Willie exercised wisdom in her public conduct. LaVona Sauters from West Virginia explained, "She really watched the way she related to people. At the time there wasn't a lot of mixing the races . . . she was respectful to others and herself. I never saw any racist in her.

"The fact she was able to go forth and preach like she did—she was just as popular in California as she was in West Virginia. The California people loved her. She touched so many people's lives and changed their views on things.

"I started school when it was segregated. As she was preaching, she was living in a segregated world, and for her to be able to pass those boundaries and be accepted like she was just amazed me. Not everybody could do that—not even in Hollywood. She was able to."

"She ministered for years mostly in southern states," said Daniel Scott, "and I can't remember her being refused by anybody. She preached for the best of them and taught in the Bible schools on ministry. They accepted her as an equal."

Kenneth Mendenhall said racial prejudice was not a problem at his church in Indiana. "Azusa Street was a black church started by a black man," said Mendenhall, "South Bend never had racial problems."

Bob Gilstrap recalled the segregation he grew up with in Oklahoma. "When I was a young teenager, there were no blacks allowed in our town as far as to stay all night and live there. Of course, we didn't agree with this, but some of the places in the South had these laws. In fact, in Oklahoma there was one town that wouldn't allow whites to stay after 6:00 p.m.

"We never had a problem in the city. Sister Willie would stay all night with us, and we just loved her tremendously."

In the early days of Sister Willie's ministry, racial segregation was the law of the land. History cannot be rewritten, but a wrong path can be corrected. In 1954, the Supreme Court made a ruling that overturned school segregation. That ruling eventually applied to other public facilities and organizations, as well. The advent of a new legal code, however, did not unilaterally affect racial prejudices held by men and women of any color. Racism remained an ongoing issue, and although vast improvements have been made, racial parity is still a work in progress.

The Civil Rights era brought much social unrest and even violence. But to the church's credit, even in the years prior to its navigation through the murky social transitions of desegregation, any civic segregation Sister Willie experienced was not carried over into the bulk of her ministry. The churches that welcomed Sister Willie did not have "white pulpits" and "colored pulpits." Neither did they have "colored toilets" or "colored fountains." Sister Willie was accepted as a person and preacher in the predominantly white congregations in which she ministered and was received without condition in the pastors's homes. She shared their tables, slept in their beds, used their facilities, and was considered family by many.

"I remember when C. L. Dees broke the color barrier and brought her to Houston, Texas, in the '60s," said Edwin Harper. "She ministered a long time before that, but there were places in the South she wasn't welcome. When Brother Dees brought her to Houston, they had such a beautiful move of God, and then Brother Fauss had her, and O. W. Williams and other churches began to use her because the move of the Holy Ghost was so splendid. She was a very graceful woman."

David Fauss of Texas said Sister Willie's biracial heritage was not an issue in his church; there were "no negative repercussions of that. We had an all-white congregation then. Today we're very diverse . . . but our people just absolutely loved her."

"Sister Willie could pass in white society in the era of segregation," noted James Stark, "because she was indeed light enough that no one would have suspected she was black. But she chose instead (because of her family) to travel with the African-American ethnicity."

Sister Willie's fair complexion enabled her to travel anywhere and be accepted. Her children, however, who were dark complected, did not have the same open access during the time of racial segregation. "That caused a lot of problems with her family, especially in the South," explained Chris Sowards, "but that wasn't so much a factor in our area."

When asked if Sister Willie suffered because of her race, David White, also from West Virginia, said, "She didn't here. I think she did other places, but Morgantown is a little unique because it started out as coal mines, then tin mills. Here now is the University of West Virginia. Most places there was an acceptance."

Although Daniel Scott affirmed Sister Willie ministered for years even in the South, he did recall one incident.

"I had one of the best choir directors you could find. He was a musician that was accomplished and doing a great job. Willie came to Open Door after he had transferred to our church. He was doing a good job—a pleasant, wonderful person.

"When I introduced Willie to the congregation, he slipped out the back door. He never did show up again during the service.

"The next time he did that, he went out my office and out the back door. I went out the front door and met him going down the walk.

"'What's your problem?' I asked him.

"'I'm not going to stay and listen,' he replied.

"I said, 'Do you have a problem with that? Then I've got a problem. I've got to find me a choir director.'

"I'm an abrupt person. I'll only take something so long before I get angry. I took him out of that position, and he and his wife went out into the world and backslid."

Dan Scott, pastor of Christ Church Nashville, knew Willie Johnson from his youth. He offered his insights:

"One of the elements to notice about Willie Johnson is how she represented the earliest generations of racially integrated Pentecostalism before regional segregation motivated the racial separation carried out by later generations of Pentecostals. She simply flew above that, not only in the North, but in the South as well.

"Her spiritual gifts transcended both the gender and racial bias of American culture. She overcame a powerful stronghold that has afflicted our nation since its beginning—not through anger, but through anointed service. People like her represent the heart of authentic spiritual life. There is so much to learn from her timeless, saintly life. She is much missed."

GENDER

"In a time when lady ministers were not popular, Sister Willie Johnson was a trailblazer," said Ginger Zimmerman. "She didn't let popular opinion stop her. She didn't let racism stop her. She didn't let small-mindedness stop her. She knew and understood her calling and her ministry. And she walked therein! As a woman in ministry, I have been preaching for thirty years and licensed with the UPCI for twenty-three years. Sister Willie Johnson is still one of my heroes of the faith!"

> "Her ministry probably was one of the most encouraging for women."
>
> —Bobbye Wendell

Sister Willie preached tent revivals with Goldie Goddard. According to Cynthia Roy, Goddard's daughter, both of the evangelists were "powerful women ministers" who "came under a lot of opposition, one for being a woman—but for Sister Willie, for being a black woman minister." Cynthia's mother told her Sister Willie never let it bother her and the two "had many services together and prayed a lot of men through to the Holy Ghost." She said, "Those two were amazing together."

"To know her was an honor," said Don Nick Ferrell. "To the ones that didn't believe in women preachers, her anointed preaching changed their minds." Jody Hussein added, "Sister Willie was a minister who loved God, preached His Word, went through much, yet kept a smile . . . I will never forget this great lady—a trailblazer for not only God, but for women."

"Nobody seemed to worry about her being a woman preacher," said David Fauss, "at least nobody in our sphere. She was just so dynamic. She didn't make a big deal out of being a woman. She was just a godly person. That was a notable time in my life. It was definitely a high point when she came and ministered—maybe three times."

"In the valley here, back in those days, women started the Apostolic movement," explained Chris Sowards. Marguerite Marple has been attributed with being the first person who brought the Oneness message to the area. Oddly enough, one man converted by Sister Marple's preaching and who was a benefactor of her ministry refused to allow Sister Willie in his pulpit because she was a woman, but this was a rare exception.[160]

RELIGION

In the early decades of Sister Willie's ministry, particularly in the 1940s and 1950s, not everyone was favorable to Pentecostalism. It was considered by some to be great fun to get drunk and tear up a Pentecostal meeting. Trouble-makers would throw rocks and beer cans and do whatever they could to disrupt worship. Unless a minister had someone on their side from the police department or mayor's office, congregations had to endure hoodlums who didn't have anything better to do than tear up a Pentecostal meeting.[161]

---

160 Per Jimmy Ramsey.
161 James Stark noted the church he grew up in was next door to a beer joint. "One time some young guys in town had too much to drink," said Stark. "They took a calf from one of the farmers and turned it loose in the vestibule of the church. It made quite a disturbance.

Sister Willie was not exempt from religious prejudice. She recalled a time she was in Moundsville playing the piano.

"God spoke to me and said, 'duck,'" said Sister Willie, "so I ducked, and a rock came through the window and hit the piano."

Sister Willie kept playing and singing.

The reason I'm in this church, I don't wanna be lost—

"The Holy Ghost said, 'duck,' and I ducked again. Every time they threw a rock, the Holy Ghost would tell me to duck, and I never got hit."[162]

Alice Torres remembered the disruptions as well. She said, "When Sister Willie would hold revivals, she knew what it was to have everything thrown at her."

Ruth Kiser gave the following tribute to Sister Willie:

"This powerful woman of God was so anointed of God and used by Him to reach thousands of people with the Gospel of Jesus Christ. She was a black woman preaching in a time of segregation, but she did not let the world and their 'opinions' dampen the Holy Ghost in her.

"She preached in season and out of season, and she did it for His glory. There will be many who will have an opportunity in eternity to thank her for letting God use her. I loved to hear her singing and preaching."

---

162 As told by James Stark and also noted in *Pioneer Pentecostal Women.*

Down from His Glory

Down from His glory
Ever living story
My God and Savior came
And Jesus was His name
Born in a manger
To His own a stranger
A man of sorrows, tears and agony
Oh, how I love Him
How I adore Him
My breath, my sunshine
My all in all
The great Creator became my Savior
And all God's fullness dwelleth in Him[163]

163 Words by William E. Booth-Clibborn, 1921; arranged from Eduardo di Capua, 1898.

Chapter 15

DOWN FROM HIS GLORY

The Johnson Children

Sister Willie gave birth to three children who lived into adulthood. Her oldest, Rudolph Jasper Johnson, was born on September 12, 1923, in Moundsville, in Marshall County, West Virginia.

Rudolph married G. Jean Mason who was born about 1926 in West Virginia. He and his family attended Emmanuel Church.[164] Rudolph was a very well-respected police officer in the city of Charleston.[165] He retired from the police department after twenty years of service, and he also retired from West Virginia's Department of Highways with fifteen years of service. Rudolph was a member of the Veterans of Foreign Wars (VFW) and the Fraternal Order of Police (FOP). He also worked at Gardner Buick.

James Stark met Rudolph as a boy and remembered him as a "good guy." He said Sister Willie called him, "My policeman boy." Daniel Scott personally knew Rudolph and regarded him as a "considerate

---

164 Chris Sowards said Rudolph was a member of Emmanuel Church. His obituary, however, mentioned he was a member of Sister Willie Johnson's Apostolic Chapel. No research has uncovered the existence of such a place.
165 Per Chris Sowards.

man." Scott said he "had a balance of being kind, but a sternness at the same time. I guess it came from being a policeman."

Rudolph and Jean had a son, Antonio, and two daughters, Donna and Barbara Ann. Rudolph died in his home after a short illness at the age of 65 on June 8, 1989, in Charleston.[166] At the time of Rudolph's passing, he also had three grandchildren and one great-grandchild. His funeral service was held at Open Door Apostolic Church and conducted by B. J. Sowards. He was buried at Sunset Memorial Park.

"Jean Johnson, though not at the same level of Sister Willie's anointing, was quite influential in the Kanawha Valley," said Chris Sowards. "She preached on the radio for many years after Sister Willie's passing, and she always honored Sister Johnson very highly. She attended our church, the Open Door, until her death in a local nursing home. Sister Jean also preached the Apostolic message and touched many lives. She always attributed any success to Sister Willie."

Scottie McKinley Johnson, the Johnson's second child, was born on December 28, 1925, also in Moundsville. In 1946 in Charleston, he married Florence Hicks who was born about 1930.[167] Bob Gilstrap recalled meeting Scottie. "Very nice looking, very personable," said Gilstrap. "We were really impressed with him." Kenneth Mendenhall called Scottie "a very nice guy, a fine man," and Larry Neal said, "He was a good light in Indianapolis."

Daniel Scott described Scottie as a "handsome, tall, well-made man," and he added, "That worried Willie, but when he married beautiful Florence, she quit worrying." Scottie and Florence had two children, Scottie and Michael.

---

166 His obituary was published in the *Charleston Gazette* on Saturday, June 10, 1989, and an amended obituary was published in the same paper on Sunday, June 11, 1989.
167 Florence passed in August 2014 in Arizona.

Sister Willie with her son, Scottie,
and daughter-in-law, Florence

Scottie Johnson, like Sister Willie, was also a minister of the gospel. Daniel Scott affirmed he was "an outstanding speaker" who "followed mostly after his mother's fantastic ministry." Although he did not generate the excitement that his mother consistently experienced, Scott said, "He was well respected in the District of West Virginia,"

Scottie was also the subject of a popular story recounted by Sister Willie, "Dirty Shirt." Allen Donham gave the following account of the "Dirty Shirt" message:

"When she was in the pulpit preaching one time, she told about her son, Scott. He had been working at his job that day—had a bad day, a bad attitude. He hardly wanted to go to church, but they talked him into it, and he threw on old clothes.

"When they got there, the minister said, 'Hey, we want you to come up and sing for us. You're always full of a great move of the Lord.'

"Scott came up and started singing, 'All day long, I've been with Jesus. It has been a glorious day. . . .'

"The point was, when he got up and started singing that song, and his shirt—he had actually put on a dirty shirt—

"Willie, in her wonderful way of telling the story, she starts singing, 'All day long I've been with Jesus (*dirty shirt, dirty shirt*), it has been (*dirty shirt, dirty shirt*) a glorious day (*dirty shirt, dirty shirt*).' She was indicating it was in his mind.

"Scott said, 'Oh, folks, I've got to stop. I've got to repent. I've had a horrible day, and I've got to repent of things I've said.' The people would laugh at that, but that was the kind of stories she told, and it would always get the point across. She was so good at that."

Later in Scottie's life, he and his family moved out west. He died at the age of 76 on January 22, 2002.

Willie and her daughter, Gloria.

Gloria Luella Johnson was born on January 24, 1927, in Moundsville. Several people remembered Sister Willie's secret code when Gloria was younger to ensure her daughter behaved herself in services. If Sister Willie shouted, "Glory!" from the platform, the people in the congregation would think she was worshipping, but her daughter knew she had better straighten up.[168]

Allen Donham recalled a story Gloria told his family when she was visiting her mother. "They would love to laugh and tell stories," said Donham. "Sister Willie told how once Gloria had a great blessing during a Holy Ghost service but a gossiper got ahold of her before they left and filled her head. Gloria said, 'You know, I just had a great service, and you filled my head with a bunch of gossip. I'm going to have to go back in there and pray through all over again.'"

"Willie was concerned for Gloria," relayed Daniel Scott. In fact, when asked Sister Willie's greatest weakness, Scott answered, "Worry about her children. She confided in us about the misgivings of her children, especially Gloria."

On the other hand, however, when asked Sister Willie's happiest moment, Scott said, "When she was with her grandchildren. She cuddled them and coddled them."[169]

Gloria wasn't always stable in her faith. Sister Willie believed her daughter had inherited some of her father's traits, but she loved her dearly. Gloria and Sister Willie were often a "package deal" when Sister Willie traveled, especially in later years.[170]

Edwin Harper recalled a time Sister Willie was talking about people who were in and out of church. It was after Gloria had gotten things right with God. "I tell you," said Sister Willie to Harper, "there will be times I see them come back to the altar, and I ask God, 'Would it be ok if I took a sledge hammer and sent them on to glory now?'"

---

168 Per Daniel Scott, Neva Limones, Karen Harding, and *Pioneer Pentecostal Women.*
169 Gracie Mitchell remembered Sister Willie's particular fondness for her grandson Scottie (also known as Chipper). "She had a grandson she was crazy about. Scottie was his name. She talked about him all the time. She loved him. I had my little son there, and she would tell me about Scottie and what he liked and didn't, and all the wonderful things about him." Larry Neal also said, "Chipper was doted over. He was a little gentleman."
170 James Stark said "In later years, any time Sister Willie came, we had to put up with Gloria and be nice to her, and she could be a real handful." He also said, "She was very jealous of her mother's anointing and how much people loved her mother."

On April 26, 1946, Gloria married Charles Robert Cole in Charleston. Information is unavailable about this relationship, except for a child, Robert Michael Cole, born June 12, 1947, in Charleston.[171] For some unknown reason, Gloria resumed life under her maiden name. Voter registration records confirm that later in life she was listed as "Miss Gloria Johnson."[172] It's unknown if the couple divorced or Charles died. Gloria passed at the age of 66 on March 11, 1993, in Santa Clara County, California.

Sister Willie's fourth son, Donald Johnson, was born November 26, 1928, and died on February 7, 1929, two months and eleven days later. He was buried at Greenlawn Cemetery in Moundsville located near the river.

---

171 Cole died in October 2002 in San Jose, California. His gravestone indicated that he was a sergeant in the U.S. army who served in Vietnam and had a daughter.
172 Per Daniel Scott.

Love Lifted Me

Verse 1

I was sinking deep in sin, far from the peaceful shore
Very deeply stained within, sinking to rise no more
But the Master of the sea heard my despairing cry
From the waters lifted me, now safe am I

Refrain

Love lifted me! Love lifted me!
When nothing else could help, Love lifted me!
Love lifted me! Love lifted me!
When nothing else could help, Love lifted me!

Verse 2

All my heart to Him I give, ever to Him I'll cling
In His blessed presence live, ever His praises sing
Love so mighty and so true merits my soul's best songs
Faithful, loving service, too, to Him belongs

Verse 3

Souls in danger look above, Jesus completely saves
He will lift you by His love out of the angry waves
He's the Master of the sea, billows His will obey
He your Savior wants to be, be saved today[173]

---

173 Words by James Rowe; music by Howard E. Smith, 1912.

Chapter 16

LOVE LIFTED ME

The 1980s

In Sister Willie's last years, she continued to minister. Randy Witt recalled a particular meeting at North Charleston Apostolic Church in the early 1980s. "I had a step-grandfather who always came to church, but I'd never seen him pray," said Witt. "He had been baptized in the '50s but never received the Holy Ghost. That night after preaching, Sister Shirley Cole went over to my papaw. He always sat in the pew behind her second-row pew. Sister Cole asked if he wanted to go up to the altar and pray.

"He curtly answered, 'No.'

"Sister Cole stood beside him nervously praying for a couple of minutes, and then turned back to him and said, 'Daddy, I'm going to ask you one more time, and I won't bother you anymore, but I believe God wants to fill you with the Holy Ghost tonight. Would you go up to the altar and pray with me?'

"He paused, said, 'Ok,' and he walked up and began to pray.

"Sister Willie came over and began to pray for him, and in just a minute or two he received the infilling of the Holy Ghost! I'll never forget her showing such compassion for a simple, old man wearing a Dickies-type work uniform."

James Stark recalled a time Sister Willie came to minister in Ohio: "A family had a little girl die of cancer. The woman was so bitter, and the family had quit coming to church. The word got out that Sister Willie was there, and for some reason that woman's bitter heart was touched and she came to the service.

"Sister Willie got up and started to sing. She walked right back to the lady. The lady just stood up, and Sister Willie put her arms around her and empathized, 'God knows, honey, God knows. And I know what it's like to lose a child. I lost one when he was two-months old,' and she went through the story."[174]

Daniel Garlitz attended one of Sister Willie's last meetings in Smithfield, Pennsylvania. "I was a home missionary there in Uniontown and was struggling in my role as a home missionary, daddy, full-time secular work, and so on. I heard she was preaching at this little country church. I attended the meeting. She didn't have a clue who I was. I was there by myself. I'd left my wife at home.

"In her preaching, she—as she normally would do—was waving her handkerchief and singing.[175] She came to the pew where I was sitting and climbed over people to get to me. I was sitting in the middle, and she got over to where I was, stuck her finger in my face and said, 'Young man, I don't know what you're going through, but the Lord told me to tell you it's going to be alright.'

---

174 This account is presumed to be the same as the one documented in *Pioneer Pentecostal Women:* "While ministering in Jewett, Ohio, in August, 1980, she felt a deep travail of Spirit. As she looked out over the congregation of nearly 300, God led her to a young couple. Discerning that they suffered an unsettled grief over the loss of a child, she ministered to their need from her own well of experience."

175 Larry Neal also remembered Sister Willie's hankies, "Beautiful lace handkerchiefs that were for more than looks."

"Then she went back on the platform. It really blessed me. She didn't give me any answers, but she gave me assurance it was going to be alright, and it was."

"The interesting thing in those days," said James Stark, "we did not understand Apostolic ministry. The gifts of the Spirit were allowed in some places, but not in others, and so people did not really understand the operation of the gifts of the Spirit and the place of the five-fold ministry in the church. And here was this woman who had a gift we didn't understand as a movement. Consequently, she had no idea what it was she had ahold of."

Stark continued, "Brother Stoneking was preaching at West Virginia Camp toward the end of her life. He told Brother Billy Cole, 'I want to meet Sister Willie. I've heard about her and never met her.'

"Brother Cole said, 'Oh, Lee, she doesn't come to camp very much. I don't know if I can get her to come.' (In those days West Virginia Camp was in Point Pleasant which was some distance away).

"Brother Stoneking said, 'Well, Billy, I want you to do everything you can to get her to come because I want to meet her.'

"She showed up that night just before Brother Stoneking was going to preach. Brother Stoneking said she walked down the aisle, they brought her to the platform, and immediately the total atmosphere in that tabernacle changed. They introduced her to the crowd and asked her to sing. She simply stood up and walked to the pulpit, lifted one hand, and shouted, 'Glory!' and miracles started to happen—immediately, simply because of the anointing of the Holy Ghost she had.

"Brother Stoneking preached that night, and afterwards they went to a truck stop. It was the only place they could go to get something to eat. There were people in there smoking, and it was a loud, noisy, dirty place. Brother Stoneking gave Sister Willie a copy of his book on the gifts of the Spirit (a little white book).

"Sister Willie came back the next night, and they went out again. She said, 'Lee, I read that book. Now I know what I have.' Until that point, she had no idea the gift she had used so effectively was the gift of the word of knowledge.

"They were sitting there that night, and Brother Cole said, 'Willie, I want you to sing.'

"She looked at him and said, 'Here?'

"'Yes.'

"'Now?'

"'Yes.'

"Sister Willie threw her head back and sang, and the atmosphere in that place immediately changed. The truck drivers fell silent. You could have heard a pin drop when she finished."

Stark also recalled a time in later years in a service in Jewett, Ohio. Pentecostal Assemblies of the World Bishop, Charles Watkins, of Cleveland, Ohio, was there. He was quite a vocal artist.

"He sang," said Stark. "He was good, real good, but Sister Willie got up to sing, and she almost took the thing over. She sang two songs, and by the time she finished, she'd prayed for half the people in the place.

"She turned to my uncle and said, 'What do you want me to do?'

"He said, 'If you're finished, Bishop Watkins is going to sing a little more.'

"She said, 'ok,' and sat down.

"The gift of faith and the gift of the word of knowledge was electrifying when Sister Willie was ministering."

Sister Willie wasn't afraid to be bold. Donna Nichols recalled her ministry at Open Door the first part of the 1980s. "I remember when she stepped on preachers' toes," said Nichols, "(as well as everyone else's), but you knew her words were directly from God!"

Allen Donham recalled the unique way Sister Willie got challenging points across to his congregation. "She walked over to the wall and said, 'You know, I was preaching down in Texas . . .' And she would put her hand over on the wall and say, 'I told those people, *even your walls are cold.*'

"The point she was making was they were cold spiritually. They were not on fire for God. She would say, 'Even your *walls* are cold.' She would get her point across, and they would understand, and they would love her for it even though they had just been preached to and their toes stepped on."

Donham was careful to add his great appreciation for Sister Willie. "She was one evangelist this pastor knew would never hurt, discourage, or say the wrong thing to the congregation."

The Lord Will Make a Way

Verse 1

Like a ship that's tossed and driven
Battered by an angry sea
When the storms of life are raging
And their fury falls on me
I wonder what I have done
That makes this race so hard to run
Then I say to my soul, take courage
The Lord will make a way somehow

Verse 2

The Lord will make a way somehow
When beneath the cross I bow
He will take away each sorrow
Let Him have your burdens now
When the load bears down so heavy
The weight is shown upon my brow
There's a sweet relief in knowing
The Lord will make a way somehow[176]

---

176 Author unknown. Recorded by Dorothy Norwood.

Chapter 17

THE LORD WILL MAKE A WAY

Willie Johnson's Legacy

During the research phase of this book, many people were asked specific questions about the legacy Sister Willie left behind. Following is a compilation of their remarks.

What advice did Sister Willie give you that made a difference in your life?

"She talked to me about ministering. She said ministry is not just a sermon. Ministering is what a minister does. It's not words. She taught me that ministry was more than just speaking—it was a heart service."

—Daniel Scott

"From the time I was a kid, she would put her hand on my shoulder and say, 'Now remember, David, your name means *blessed of the Lord,* and God has called you for a great work.'

"The last time I saw her, she was in town and she called me. We sat down and talked, and she said, 'Oh, my God, Son, what has happened to the church? It's a sign of the times. Don't follow this. You keep to the truth you've known since you were a child.'"

—David White

What was her greatest strength?

"Her ability to follow the leading of the Holy Spirit."

—Michell Cole

"Her spiritual insight. Her stamina to take a stand regardless of what she went through."

—Edwin Harper

"Her sensitivity to be used in the gift of the word of knowledge."

—James Stark

"Her discernment."

—Kenneth Mendenhall

"She had a mainline to God. I can say without any hesitation, her strength was drawing her ministry direct from the throne. It was 'hot bread' always. She could use the same Scripture and preach one hundred messages from it, and they would never be the same."

—Daniel Scott

What is your favorite Sister Willie quote or a verse she quoted often?

"She once told my mom, who was having difficulties with another pastor's wife, 'Pray for them. It might not help them, but it will help you.' This quote has been re-quoted to me many times in my life.

"I had a deep respect for Sister Willie. I would listen to her if she would speak to me, even in rebuke, if necessary."

—Neva Limones

"Don't be a garbage can, saints."

—Larry Neal

"'Honey, you can make it,' and 'Trust in God.' She would say, 'Humans may fail, but God never fails you.'"

—Allen Donham

"She used a lot of the time, the 23rd Psalm, 'Yea, though I walk through the valley of the shadow. . . . ' She was not talking about death, but difficulties. She would stop and say, 'Yea, though I walk through the valley. . . .'"

—Daniel Scott

What did you admire most about Sister Willie?

"I admired most the fact that she had so much connection with God. I had not seen it on that scale at all—to see her operate ministering to people. Once she got my attention, I was always there whenever she was in town."

—Roger Zimmerman

"She was a woman who walked with a great gift of power in her presence. Her life showed (through suffering and faith), the power the Lord can trust a person with."

—Christine Martinez

"She was powerful and as kind as she could be. Some people who are gifted aren't very nice, and she was not that. You could sum her up with Proverbs 31—*The Virtuous Woman*."

—Chris Sowards

"She was a most beautiful woman. She carried herself with dignity. She was honest and sincere, and she was kind."

—Neva Limones

"I had never seen such a moving of God's Spirit before. I realized women of God were powerful."

—Michell Cole

"Her sincerity. She was transparent. If she didn't like something, she let you know. She let me know lots of times."

—Daniel Scott

What do you feel was the most important thing she did?

"She really loved people. She never used them. She treated all equally no matter if they were 'high up' or just ignorant, unlearned people. Everyone was a soul."

—Neva Limones

"The most important thing she did in her ministry— she ministered."

—Bob Gilstrap

"She ministered to the hurt—to the heart—to the broken."

—Daniel Scott

"She made everyone feel like they were her best friend."

—Edwin Harper

"Encouraged."

—Allen Donham

"Communication and the faith to carry it through. She was a builder of faith."

—Bobbye Wendell

How did she make you feel?

"She made you feel as if you were the most important person in the world. Her eyes were so deep and warm. She was like Christ would be if He were in the flesh among us. In church, you wanted to hear what was going to be said. We wanted to be still and not miss anything, even though we were children."

—Neva Limones

"I loved her. I remember feeling like she was very special and I was very fortunate to really be on the inside track with her since she would stay at my grandparent's house. I got to be around her. I looked at her like she was a celebrity."

—Lois Truman

"She made you feel special. When we're with some people, it's all about them. I've remarked to my wife that many people, when you talk to them, instead of being a good conversationalist, they want to talk about what they're doing. They never ask you, 'How are you doing? How's your ministry? What are you feeling from the Lord now? How are your kids?'

"I have one friend who does that—but some people are so focused on themselves they only think of themselves, so you don't feel important in their midst. Sister Willie made you feel comfortable, like family, important—not 'out of the way' with 'high blown' compliments—just the way she treated you. You felt you were important—vital."

—Bob Gilstrap

"She made me feel like I was very important—like I was something far more than what I should have thought of myself. She elevated me even in her ministry in our church— to heights that I did not climb.

"It wasn't because she was exaggerating—that's what she really felt, because she loved me as a pastor. She loved me as a man of God, and she had a companion spirit with me.

"When we were together, we talked about spiritual things—except the times she got off on something funny."

—Daniel Scott

How did Sister Willie personally impact your life?

"Other than my parents, I think no one influenced my life like Sister Willie. Although I was so young, I knew the power of God that I felt—the way He moved—how I felt.

"Her songs are so deeply ingrained in the fiber of my being. Every time in my life I've gone through severe difficulties, those are the words I sing. They lift my spirit, and help me to remember God is with me. I know for myself, I would not have made it sometimes had I not had memories of her ministry. Her songs have sustained me many times.

"When I minister in Word or song, I aspire to be like her, that it be from my heart and honest. I want my life to be like her in that I practice what I preach and that I be truthful always."

—Neva Limones

"She was just such a dynamic woman, and she did make me want to be closer to the Lord. When people heard her, they were compelled.

"She was one of a kind, and I will never forget her. I wish there were more women evangelists like her. Women have a place in the church that is so underutilized, and it's sad, because I think in the first-century church, there were quite a few women who had roles, and I think the Lord wants to do that. I would really like to see ladies in the church fulfill their calling. The body of Christ needs that special sensitivity."

—William Finn

"I had a problem with a lady in our church, and I had to be a little rough with her. As a pastor's wife, I felt it was my right to tell her, but Sister Willie caught wind of it because she was at our church.

"I said, 'Sister Willie, tell me, how can I heal this situation?'

"The woman and I had been close friends. 'Now she won't even speak to me,' I said. 'She won't come around. She won't even come to church at times because she was so upset.'

"Sister Willie said, 'Let me tell you something. I know her. I know what she is. Just leave her alone. She'll get over it and come back and it will be like it was.' And it was."

—Joy Scott

"I loved her and thought she was the most used woman of God I had ever seen."

—Michell Cole

"She was my best friend. Willie was my anchor to a greater spiritual level than I had already known. My mother was the second person in our area baptized in Jesus's name. She had the Holy Ghost all those years, and she told me, 'You can preach without praying, but you cannot minister without praying.'"

"My mom taught me that God's time (and I still honor it) is from 5:00 a.m. to 6:00 a.m. every morning. That's my prayer time. And that's where I draw my strength. I was a praying person long before I met Willie, but she taught me. She was an anchor to the more spiritual values of ministry.

"When she would be ministering, things would go so beautifully, and I would be sitting there almost with my chin in my hand listening intently. I never remember a time I felt she was going long or overdoing her time. She would turn to me and talk to me apart from the congregation and say things to me. Her words were always encouraging me to minister to the brokenhearted. She always ministered to me and told me to represent Jesus Christ."

—Daniel Scott

"The ministry of Evangelist Willie Johnson was unique and needed for God's people in the day and hour she was with us on this earth. It is needed today and sorely missed. God, raise up women who will allow themselves to be used and sold out for You in these last days and hours."

—Linda McGinnis

If there was one word you could use to describe her, what would it be?

Angelic—Randy Witt

Anointed—William Finn and David White

Caring—Dorothy Nalley

Deep—Allen Donham

Gifted—Edwin Harper

God-chosen—Rosalee Donham

Godly—Joy Scott

Power—Tom Foster

Powerful—Michell Cole and Jimmy Ramsey

Power-packed—Elizabeth Lopez

Real—Bob Gilstrap and Roger Zimmerman

Refreshing—David Fauss

Revivalist—Douglas Rashall

Righteous—Neva Limones

Spontaneous (in the Spirit)—Lois Truman

Unforgettable—Daniel Scott

Unique—Chris Sowards

If Sister Willie were writing her story, what would she want us to remember about her or learn from her life?

"That God did it. She was not a boaster. She never said 'I' did this or 'I' did that. It was about 'God' did that."

—LaVona Sauters

"Fast and pray and live for Jesus every day like her song says."
—Neva Limones

"In spite of difficulty and opposition and disappointments and tragedies, God is with you. He loves you. He's faithful. Hang in there. She was an encourager. She was an uplifter, a supporter. That was just really her ministry. I think that would be her desire—to encourage people."
—Bob Gilstrap

"She (like David) was a woman after God's own heart."
—Allen Donham

"Her walk with God."
—Michell Cole

"She loved people. She genuinely loved people, and consequently people loved her."
—James Stark

"She was totally and completely sold out and surrendered to the Lord, and I think she would teach people to be that same way—completely sold out."
—William Finn

"Probably more than anything else, she was a servant. She was a servant of the Lord. It didn't matter what God impressed her to do, she would do it—no *ifs, ands,* or *buts.* She was very faithful to the Kingdom of God. She never felt she was any less because of her background. She was just a human being on equal footing with everyone else, and they treated her that way."
—David White

"You can walk with the Lord no matter what the enemy or anyone else sends your way. You just be faithful, and He will see you through it."

—Randy Witt

"She would want us to remember that it was God's ministry, and she was a vessel that He chose to use. She was totally sold out to God.

—Roger Zimmerman

"She would want us to remember she did what she could to pray people through to the Holy Ghost. The old church was a little different than today—church 'til midnight or one in the morning—and she'd be right there at the altar tarrying with people. In and out of the pulpit, it was about souls."

—Chris Sowards

"She loved God enough to suffer for Him. She would often say that it's not about the joys, it's about the tears that turn you into a good Christian."

—Edwin Harper

"That God will use any vessel that is completely devoted to the Spirit. When your focus is on Kingdom-building and Kingdom-mindedness, it doesn't matter who you are or anything about you. God will use you in a mighty way."

—Lois Truman

"How good God is. How she came through so much—that God saw her through it. Her face would just shine when she talked about Jesus. She was in a different world when she was talking about Jesus. She was actually *not* in the pulpit—she was in the very heaven of heavens. She taught me how to minister."

—Daniel Scott

"She would want people to remember that God was a provider. Through trials and tribulations, He's still holding your hand."
—Kenneth Mendenhall

"Her depth of spirituality made her a spiritual giant."
—Allen Donham

Dorothy Nalley summed up Sister Willie's ministry by saying, "Her testimony and her songs emphasized that no matter what you are going through in life, He is there. He won't fail you. He will be a light in darkness and bread when we are hungry.

"She had that testimony, and she emphasized that no matter what situation we find ourselves in, He is only a prayer away."

Missionary Bobbye Wendell spoke with conviction in her voice when she said, "What Willie Johnson manifested is where we need to go back in Pentecost today and reignite. The brokenness, the submission, and not building any kind of 'kingdom' for ourselves, but ministering to people. You can find faith and positive preaching, but the brokenness that she manifested is not a real obvious thing. That was her type of ministry. That brokenness—it's hard to find anymore."

Dan Scott, pastor of Christ Church Nashville, in remembering Sister Willie's ministry, expressed his hopes that "a new generation can reconnect to something that is far more than volume, clever turns of phrase, marketing, and entrepreneurial machinery. The early Pentecostal movement was good news to the poor and deliverance from the strongholds of evil. We can find our way to that again."

Just What Heaven Means to Me

Verse 1

A place where there is no misunderstanding
And from all enmity and strife we're free
And where no unkind words are ever spoken
Oh, that is just what heaven means to me

Refrain

What will it be when we get over yonder
And meet our loved ones who've gone before
What joy 'twill be to see our blessed Savior
Oh, that is just what heaven means to me

Verse 2

A home where there is no more trouble
And where we're free from sickness death and war
Eternal joy and peace will be forever
Oh, that is just what heaven means to me [177]

---

177 Above lyrics recorded by Willie Johnson. Original words and music by Jimmie Davis, 1974.

Chapter 18

JUST WHAT HEAVEN MEANS TO ME

The Last Years

Sister Willie did not like to fly. She preferred, instead, to take the train.[178] During her lifetime, she was involved in two different Amtrak train accidents. In one of them, the car she was in went underwater. She could have drowned, but God kept her safe. As she waited in the train, she sang, "Some through the waters, some through the flood."[179]

In May of 1981, Sister Willie traveled with her daughter Gloria to California. Weakness settled in and worsened over several weeks. As her health failed, Sister Willie expected she would not be long for this world.

"When I got here, to San Jose," said Sister Willie, "I was sick, and the doctor said a few weeks later, I would have been gone—one lung had collapsed. I had a tumor the size of a woman five months pregnant, plus two the size of cantaloupes, two the size of lemons. They called in a medical team, and it made medical history. The twelve-pound tumor had been growing twenty years. Oh, how great God is!"[180]

---

178 Per Gracie Mitchell.
179 Per Edwin Harper, Gracie Mitchell, and Linda McGinnis.
180 Quote from *Pioneer Pentecostal Woman*.

Sister Willie said she cried for months to die and go home to be with her Lord, but she had to accept that He wanted her to stay awhile longer. "He knows the way we take," she said, "and when He has tried us, we shall come forth as gold. Above everything, hold to His hand, hold on, hold to God's unchanging hand."[181]

After Sister Willie's surgery, she did very little preaching, but she did minister in the first part of the decade, and people still flocked to hear her. "When word got out Sister Willie was coming," said James Stark, "the people would pack the church—I mean pack it. People would come who had been backslidden for years and bring money like you could not believe."

By this time Gloria traveled with her mother everywhere. Sister Willie said it was so Gloria could take care of her, but Sister Willie was taking care of Gloria, too.

"The offerings would be off the charts for Sister Willie," said Stark. "The last time she came to preach for us, I was the assistant pastor and my uncle the pastor. At the end (of I believe three services) we had thousands of dollars that had come in for her.

"She had mentioned that she was behind with her dues to the West Virginia District. My uncle said, 'If you'd like me to, I'll send that directly to the district.'"

It had come to the minister's attention that when the offerings were given directly to Sister Willie, someone else always seemed to get ahold of the money. Stark said the pastor asked Sister Willie, "Do you have any other bills I can pay for you?" The elderly lady gave him a number of bills she needed paid—utility bills she was behind on. "The church wrote checks directly to those needs," said Stark, "and there was still money left.

"My uncle, Hugh Rose, said, 'If I give all this to her, it will be gone.'" Rose knew Sister Willie wasn't very good at managing money and others were good at spending the money she earned.

---

181 Ibid.

Stark continued, "We gave her a huge offering for a week and put the rest in an account marked 'Sister Willie,' and every month we sent her a check. That went on for some time.

"My mother was the church secretary, and she said one day, 'Well, we've got one more check left for Sister Willie, and then all that money will be gone.'

"I think we sent her $100 or $150 a month for over a year. When my mom wrote the last check, she was crying when she put it in the mailbox because she knew Sister Willie needed that money. Sister Willie died before the check got there, and the family returned that check. It was the most amazing thing. They hadn't received it in time to cash it before she died. and they returned it.

"My wife and I went to see her three days before she died," said Stark.[182] "She was in the hospital in Charleston, and we went to see her. She was unconscious. I don't think she knew we were there.

"I remember going into her hospital room, and I'd never seen her look weak until then. She obviously had been weaker—kind of stooped toward the end—but when she would begin to minister, she would come alive. She would throw that hand in the air and something happened."

"She wasn't able to travel a whole lot in the last years. The church had moved and the building was a mess, but she was there preaching. There was plywood and light bulbs hanging out of the ceiling. That's where they made her her own apartment.

"When she was there, lives changed. The culture has changed today. Revival now is maybe a Friday and Sunday services. Back in those days, it would be week after week, and she would go and go and go. Even at the end, as weak as she was, when the anointing would come on her, she would transform into this other person like she'd been in the past. She transformed into superwoman, preached for an hour, ministered at the

---

182 Allen Donham and his wife, Jeanne, were also able to visit Sister Willie in the hospital before she passed.

altar an hour, and then she would buckle over again and be like an old lady. People would have to help her in and out of her car.

"Outside of the pulpit, Willie loved to laugh. She loved to eat. She had suffered abuse . . . but she never complained. She was very close to my folks. Those last twenty years of her life I'm really grateful my parents looked out for her.

"She never had much. I'd heard people talk about her 'driving around in a big old Cadillac,' but it was big and junkie. There was nothing pretentious about her. She had an old 1969 two-door Cadillac. I don't know where she got it, but she was so proud of it. She had someone paint it red, her favorite color. She would drive around town when she was old in that car, and she shouldn't have been. Whenever she couldn't get in traffic and she didn't think she'd fit, she'd close her eyes and say, 'In Jesus's name' and go through."

According to a booklet made commemorating the Open Door Apostolic Church's 60th anniversary, Sister Willie held her last revival in her home church before she passed.

Excerpt from the Open Door Apostolic Church's 60th anniversary booklet:

Another exciting thing happened during that time that would forever change the lives of those who were a part of the Open Door. It was during September of 1940 that Evangelist Willie Johnson began making Open Door her home. To know Sister Johnson was to love her, for truly she was one of the most anointed ministers of this century, and yet she was humble. You would have to search far and wide to find a greater soul winner than Sister Willie Johnson. In fact, there are men and women, pastors and evangelists, preachers and saints alike around this country that came to God because of the ministry of Sister Johnson. Yet, for all of the places she went, there was no place she loved more than the place that she called home, and that was Open Door. A value could never be placed upon the legacy that this great lady left to our church, nor could it ever be summed up in words, the impact that she had on so many lives.

The West Virginia District was home to Sister Willie Johnson all her life, and the District has been honored to call Sister Willie Johnson one of their pioneers. Sister Willie was also proud to be a West Virginian. At United Pentecostal Church General Conferences years ago, districts gathered for group pictures, and Sister Willie always made it a point to have her picture made with the West Virginia ministers.[183]

"The tumor returned, and she was hospitalized," said Daniel Scott. "Rudolph's wife, Jean, called me several times to tell me she was in the hospital. I would visit Sister Willie.

"The last time I had just got in from a long ministry trip—perhaps overseas. Jean called me and told me, 'Brother Scott, Willie has gone into a coma. She's been into a coma for about three days. She doesn't recognize or respond to anybody, any voice, any touch.'

"I went up there, and the family talked to me. Jean said, 'Brother Scott, she won't know you, but (I remember what she said so vividly) she loves you so. Would you go in and pray with her?'

"I walked to the door, and Jean and some of the others followed me. I said, 'Mama Willie, how are you doing?'

"Her face was turned away from me. When I spoke, she turned around. I don't think she ever focused on me. Her eyes were sort of glazed, looking nowhere.

"She recognized my voice and said, 'Daniel Scott, a man in whom there is no guile nor shadow of turning.' Then she turned back over and didn't say any more.

"The family was amazed. And I think that was the last time she spoke."

---

183 Per Edwin Harper.

Sister Willie passed from this life on January 24, 1984, in the Charleston Area Medical Center in Charleston, West Virginia. Her funeral services were held in the Open Door Apostolic Church in Charleston, where she had been a member for many years. Because of responsibilities in the Jewett church, James Stark and his uncle could not both attend the funeral. Since Stark had gone to see her in the hospital, his uncle went, and James heard about the funeral through the reports of others.

"Billy Cole and R. L. Mitchell both told me this story individually," said Stark. "The night before her funeral there were a number of people who had come in from all over the country. There were two or three older black ladies playing the piano and singing. People were just visiting, and all of a sudden the ladies at the piano stopped.

"There was a hush that fell over the whole place. There were over one hundred people there. Brother Cole and Brother Mitchell both said the place got deathly silent.

"Brother Mitchell leaned up and said to Brother Billy Cole, 'This place is full of angels.'

"Brother Cole said, 'I know. They've come to pay their respects.'

"For several minutes no one said a word and no one moved. The angels left, and both of them told me they'd never experienced anything like that before in their lives—such a vividly strong angelic visitation."

At her funeral, special singing and music were presented by Brother and Sister Hugh Rose and Sister Helen Claytor. They sang, 'His Eye is on the Sparrow,' 'To God Be the Glory,' 'Amazing Grace,' and 'God Leads Us Along.'

Robert Mitchell of Houston, Texas, opened with prayer.

B. J. Sowards, the pastor of the Open Door Church at the time, gave the eulogy.

Billy Cole gave a personal tribute and read some of the telegrams received, including the following from the General Superintendent of the United Pentecostal Church International:

Willie Johnson—saint of God; preacher deluxe; singer extraordinary; God's chosen has fought the fight, kept the faith, and gained the crown.

The contribution she made to the church is beyond measure. She breathed her life into the fellowship of the United Pentecostal Church, and the life she breathed gave life to those that were dead in transgression.

She stands in the presence of Almighty God with sheaves in her hand. She was a soul winner, an intercessor. Nothing greater could be said about any one person.

Heaven rejoices! The Victor has conquered and come home. We are left behind mourning her departure and praying for her dear loved ones who will miss this beautiful, shining light.

Sister Urshan and all the headquarters personnel join with me in extending our sympathy and also our deepest respect.

—Nathaniel Urshan
General Superintendent
United Pentecostal Church International

James Kilgore of Houston, Texas, an Assistant Superintendent of the United Pentecostal Church and a long-time friend of Sister Willie, said he represented "some 7,000 ministers, some 3,500 churches, some 263 missionaries, and a long line of believers who could rise up and say, 'Sister Willie, you blessed me.'"

Kilgore delivered a heartfelt message, "An Elect Lady," in which he remarked Sister Willie might stand alongside great people of the Bible such as Ruth, Miriam, and Mary. He envisioned the psalmist David saying to Sister Willie, "Let me teach you how to play the harp," and when they finished, Sister Willie might say, "Now David, let me teach you how to sing!"

Kilgore reminded the people of Sister Willie's inspiring example in attitude, in suffering, in simplicity, in motherhood, as a minister, as a prophetess, and more. He said, "She knew the power of a song and never lost her power to sing."

Norman Mills, West Virginia District Superintendent of the United Pentecostal Church International, offered the closing remarks and prayer.

It was told to James Stark by Billy Cole that on the day of Sister Willie's funeral it was clear a certain woman had determined to make some kind of a scene. James Kilgore was preaching and Billy Cole was sitting on the platform. The woman began to stand and Cole knew she was getting ready to interrupt the funeral. Stark related the story, "Brother Cole said she got about halfway up out of her seat, and he said, 'I curse you in Jesus's name.'

"He didn't say it loud, but she froze there, and she was unable to stand up or sit down. She just stayed there until finally she was able to sit down and didn't say another word the rest of the funeral."

"The sanctuary had three skylights," said Chris Sowards. "The day of her funeral, it was a dark, rainy day outside; and when Brother Hugh Rose got up and began to sing, a ray of sunlight came through just one window and started shining on the casket."

Kenneth Mendenhall confirmed this peculiar phenomenon. "When they opened the funeral that day, it was like somebody turned a spotlight from heaven on her casket. There were three windows, and light came only through one."

"I'm convinced this lady was so powerful in the Spirit that God did indeed send angels to her funeral and to that wake the night before."

—James Stark

Sister Willie's pallbearers were Robert Mitchell, E. C. Sowards, Hubert Fowler, Allen Donham, Kenneth Mounts, and Ronald Moss. Every minister present was considered an honorary pallbearer, and the ministers' wives served as flower bearers.

Sister Willie Johnson was laid to rest in Sunset Memorial Park on MacCorkle Avenue SW in South Charleston, West Virginia. Her dear friend and pastor, Daniel Scott, arrived in Charleston from an extended trip to Canada just in time for the closing prayer at the cemetery.

"When my wife told me she passed," said Scott, "I cancelled everything I was doing in Canada and flew home, but it was too late for the funeral. I got there just in time to offer the closing prayer at Sister Willie's graveside and say goodbye to her."

At the time of her death, Evangelist Willie Lane Johnson was survived by her children Rudolph, Scottie, and Gloria, as well as one sister, Anna Mae Reynolds of Roanoke, Virginia, seven grandchildren and six great-grandchildren. Her life left an imprint on thousands of others, and through this work, hopefully, on generations to come.

Left: Willie in her golden years.
Right: Grave Marker.

In 2002, Sister Willie Johnson was inducted into the Order of the Faith, the United Pentecostal Church International's prestigious award honoring outstanding achievement and exemplary service to the church. David Fauss, who chaired the committee that recommended her, said, "Every person who ever heard her minister was impacted by her."

EPILOGUE

A t the conclusion of months of research, interviews, and writing, I've come to know Sister Willie Johnson through the memories and testimonies of others. As I worked, I felt a kinship with her and a deep stirring in my spirit.

She's alive, I can tell you that. And I don't know if she has that recliner in heaven she asked for, but I'm sure of one thing—she still has her song.

When people looked at the woman in the cape, they saw Willie Johnson, but they felt God. I realized early in the research phase of this project that *Through the Waters* is more than the "Willie story." It's the "Jesus story." It's a testimony to what God can do in and through a broken, sold-out vessel.

Sister Willie's approach to suffering was unique. She believed trials were blessings in disguise. She did not try to avoid suffering, but she genuinely believed and preached that if God chose a person to suffer, He would give sufficient grace with each challenge. She believed it was a privilege to suffer for His name's sake. It was because of this paradigm she was able to bear her challenges with dignity.

She faced hate with love, anger with gentleness, and pain with prayer and praise; and in doing so, she obtained a deep, rich, dynamic ministry. Willie Johnson traded her sorrows for the joy of the Lord, and God transformed her sufferings into a ministry that brought glory to Him and healing to others.

Sister Willie was so full of God, His Spirit spilled out of her and splashed onto the people she met. She was so full of the love of Jesus, she couldn't keep it to herself. She had an anointing and a way of conducting herself that has inspired me, and I hope will continue to inspire others.

When I reflected on my takeaways from "knowing" Sister Willie through the writing of her biography, three thoughts surfaced and have remained at the top:

Rise above your circumstances.

Rejoice.

Good triumphs over evil.

I've been reminded and hope to remind every reader that although the demoralizing effects of rejection, abuse, and harsh circumstances are real and crippling, they can be overcome by the love of God. As an ordained minister with the United Pentecostal Church International, Sister Willie has posthumously challenged me. Her depth of spirituality has drawn me to a deeper place in God, and I see so clearly—although there could never be another like her—our generation needs its own Willie Johnsons.

At the beginning of 2018, during my personal devotion, the Lord impressed words into my spirit that have echoed in my heart and mind for over a year.

Dormant seed will be awakened and reactivated.

I knew immediately God was referring to some who had lost their way with Him, and that it also included those who had grown cold on the pew. As I pondered more deeply, I realized there is dormant seed also in the heart of every believer—no matter how passionately that person loves and serves God. The seed of the Holy Ghost that is deposited in the life of His children has not yet done all it is able to do, nor have we fulfilled all God desires. There is more of God to experience. And until He comes to take us home, there is more work to do for His kingdom.

Sister Willie envisioned her recliner in heaven, but we are not yet at the end of our journeys. It's not time for us to *recline*. It is time to *incline*—to incline our hearts to the heart of God and hear the message Sister Willie's life still preaches: Love God. Love people. The Spirit beckons us to to live in the moment with Him and live consecrated to Him so we can hear His voice, move in the Spirit, and touch people with the transforming power of God's love.

Sister Willie was sold out. If our generation is going to see the type of Spirit-led ministry that brings true inner healing and hope, God's children (especially those called to ministry) must sell out in the same way.

The Spirit of the Living God is speaking life to dormant seed even now. He's resurrecting and reactivating gifts; and He is reigniting passion for true, pure, selfless ministry.

NOTES & CONTRIBUTORS

Through the Waters is a creative compilation of research and memories that reflects the present recollections of long-ago experiences. As I poured through research and conducted interviews, a few recollections conflicted (primarily of locations and timing). I have done my best to vet information and paint a truthful story; but this is a book of memories, and memories, at times, may unwittingly obscure details.

I would like to thank everyone who spoke with me or provided information. Quotations are those received or recorded elsewhere and are not represented in some cases as word-for-word transcripts. The essence of any recreated or retold dialogue is considered to be accurate.

The details of personal accounts are those of the individuals who documented them, shared them, or who contributed them to the public record. If there are any errors or omissions, I cannot assume responsibility for them. I did take the liberty to correct grammar and punctuation as well as switch pronouns with personal names to improve readability.

Special thanks to Daniel and Joy Scott, James Stark, Edwin Harper, and Allen Donham. Much appreciation goes to Neva Limones, who not only contributed to the book, but at times I felt she was my personal assistant on the project. Thanks to pre-publication readers for their input and help polishing the manuscript, including Karen Hemmes, Vonelle Kelly, Daniel Koren, Tiffany Main, and Beth Smith.

I'd like to acknowledge the following organizations and their representatives:

Apostolic Archives

Apostolic Bible Institute

Center for the Study of Oneness Pentecostalism

Christian Life College

Texas Bible College.

Finally, thanks to all who were interviewed or otherwise shared their memories of the life and ministry of Sister Willie Johnson:

Adams, George

Aikey, Harold*

Angeles, Jeneen*

Ballard, Sharri

Ballestero, Martyn

Barnes, Charlene

Barnett, Buddy

Bass, Ernest

Bernardini, John

Bickford, Ruby

Brian, Ronald

Bruner, Mary June

Butler, Shaun

Chance, Wylma Ruth*

Clemons, Whitley

Cobbler, Brenda

Cohron, Pat

Cole, Billy & Shirley*

Cole, Michell Anderson

Cummings, Shelly

Day, Dan

DeFord, Maurice

Demos, Alan

Donham, Allen

Donham, Bob & Rosalee

Dove, Della

Duhe, Marilyn Harrod

Fauss, David

Ferrell, Don Nick*

Finn, William

Foster, Tom

Fowler, Andrew*

Ganey, Charlie*

Garlitz, Daniel

Gilstrap, Bob

Glasco, Frank

Glosson, Aretta Grisham*

Goss, Betty*

Harding, Karen

Harper, Ed & Sharon

Harrah, Debby Lawrence

Haymon, Donald

Herring, Wayne E.

Holland, Joe

Huffman, Sandee

Hussein, Jody Henderson

Johnson, Janice*
Johnson, Scottie (Chipper)
Johnson, Tom
Jones, Debra Perine*
Jordan, J. Mark*
Kelbaugh, Albert*
Keefer, Brenda*
Kirchner, Kelli*
Kiser, Ruth
Kitchen, Debbie
Klinedinst, Doug
Laird, Robin
Leaman, Jack
Limones, Neva
Lopez, Elizabeth
Malik, Dreama
Mangun, Vesta
Martin, Don
Martin, Margaret
Martin, Martha Ann*
Martinez, Christine
McBride, Darrell G.
McGinnis, Linda Lea
McGray, Donna
Mendenhall, Kenneth
Meyer, David
Mitchell, Gracie
Morgan, Kenneth
Nalley, Dorothy Uldean*
Napier, Crystal A.
Neal, Larry
Nichols, Donna*
Nicholson, Sandra*
Pate, Randall

Place, Roxanna*
Price, Jarrod
Ramsey, Dave
Ramsey, Delores
Ramsey, Jimmy
Rashall, Douglas
Reavis, Jan*
Reynolds-Rice, Tammy
Roy, Cynthia Goddard
Sauters, LaVona
Sayer, Kim Eskew
Scott, Daniel & Joy
Scott, Dan, Jr.
Shanzer, Teresa
Showalter, David
Simmons-Garcia, Deborah*
Snead, Michael Stephen
Snider, Diana
Sowards, Chris
Sowards, Carolyn*
Sowards, Margie*
Stanley, Adrian
Stark, James
Starkey, Nancy*
Starr, Dorothy
Stoneking, Lee*
Stoops, Rick
Strickland, Jerry*
Strickland, Sim
Tatum, Gene
Torres, Alice
Trout, Wayne & Janet
Truman, Lois
Turley, Lynn*

Underwood, Teresa
Wales, Judy
Wallace, Mary*
Watts, Deanna
Weldy, Sherry
Wendell, Bobbye
West, Wanda*
White, David
Williams, Linda*

Willis, Eileen*
Wilson, Mary
Wilson, Tammy
Witt-Means, Cindy
Witt, Randy
Yonts, Jack*
Ziemke, Lorraine*
Zimmerman, Ginger
Zimmerman, Roger

*These were from written accounts or audio/video accounts. Attempts were made to contact living contributors for permission to use their memories or testimonies shared publicly elsewhere.

RESOURCE LIST

Books:

Apostolic Bible Institute Yearbook, Edited by Nathan Stewart, Tracy Claunch, Eleanor Grant, Joanne Swim, Ann Grant, Brenda Schreffler, Paula Warren, Michael Harrell, John Starks, Jim Smith, Joe Holland, Dennis Mast, Richard Hinkle, Anthony Labunski, Richard Swearingen, Dennis Killman, Gary Gossett, George Szozda, John Sides, Terrence Weinkauf, Mark Edge and Bill Chapman (St. Paul, MN: Apostolic Bible Institute, 1987).

Pioneer Pentecostal Women, vol. 2, compiled by Mary H. Wallace (Hazelwood, MO: Word Aflame Press, 1981).

Our Historical Stepping Stones of the West Virginia District, compiled and edited by Daniel Scott (Hazelwood, MO: Word Aflame Press, 2008).

Periodicals:
Pentecostal Herald
Pentecostal Outlook
West Virginia District News
Lubbock Avalanche-Journal
Morgantown Post
Athens Messenger
The *Odessa American*

Muncie Evening Press
The *Indianapolis Star*

Sister Willie's Song Books & Albums
Willie Johnson Youtube & Myspace Channels
Public Records (Death Certificate, Census Records)
Order of Faith Induction
Funeral Program

The Story Behind the Story of Sister Willie's New Birth Experience

Chapter 1 is a dramatization of Sister Willie's new birth experience. It was written based on the information provided by many people who heard bits and pieces of her story over the years. It is what I believe to be most accurate, although I cannot claim the account represents Sister Willie's complete conversion story.

The details of Sister Willie's coming to faith were provided by contributors who personally knew and heard her speak about her testimony. Daniel Scott, Linda McGinnis, James Stark, Edwin Harper, and Delores Ramsey were primary contributors.

Daniel Scott knew Sister Willie from 1947 until her death, served as her pastor, and was a close friend and confidante. He became her pastor in 1958, in the years of her ministry as a widow, and during those years she confided in him much of the heartbreak she had suffered.

The details Daniel Scott shared have been substantiated by others including being spoken by Sister Willie in services at the Open Door Church in Charleston. In fact-checking for a reference to the bridge in Moundsville, I found only a four-lane bridge that was built in 1986, but Daniel Scott worked as a riverboat pilot in the 1950s and attested to the existence of a previous bridge that he had piloted his boat under a multitude of times. In full disclosure, Daniel Scott had written at one time that Sister Willie witnessed to Bud, but he later verified it was Bud Entsminger who was preaching in Moundsville when she passed by the church.

Allen Donham knew Sister Willie for decades and spent extended amounts of time with her as she regularly visited and stayed in the parsonage next to their church in her final years. "She would talk to us during the day, and a lot of things were given to us at that time that really were not for the public," said Donham. He aptly stated in his interview, "We have bits and pieces of her conversion. She would tell it to us over time; however, to give complete accuracy and dates and all that is going to be—you'll have to read between the lines of your different testimonies."

Edwin Harper grew up in Morgantown and later pastored the Morgantown church. He knew Sister Willie all his life. She stayed in the Harper home. The account of the women coming from Morgantown was told to Edwin Harper by Ruth Fisher, who was a member of the church he pastored and who was also one of the four women involved in the incredible intervention by the Lord in the mid-1920s.

James Stark lived with his grandparents until fifth grade, and Sister Willie stayed in their home when he was a boy. He heard Sister Willie tell stories at the dinner table and while sitting around visiting after church. His mother, Ella May, was a close friend of Sister Willie for decades.

Miscellaneous notes of Sister Willie's conversion story:

Willie Lane Cougar was born in Roanoke, Virginia, on May 2, 1905. Three people who knew Sister Willie well recalled her telling her father was a famous senator, and one person specifically mentioned Tennessee. A record of Daniel Layne's service in this public office in Tennessee coincides with the timing.

The age discrepancy between Willie and Scott Johnson was verified by the 1940 census. Scott Johnson was born in 1880 in Alabama, the son of William and Elxeia Johnson.

Willie Johnson's conversion story was recorded in *Pioneer Pentecostal Women* compiled by Mary Wallace. It was included in this account that Sister Willie first had an encounter with a woman in a cemetery who had changed Sister Willie's mind about suicide. Some time afterwards, the account had Sister Willie attending the Pentecostal church out of curiosity to see the evangelist (Bud Entsminger) lift the Bible stand while he was preaching.

There have been other accounts that Sister Willie received the Holy Ghost in a woman's kitchen.

The version dramatized in *Through the Waters* includes details remembered by many people during the research for this book. It is not presented as the complete story, but it is what the author believes to be most accurate.

APPENDIX II

"Through the Waters" Album Dedication by Willie Johnson

In shady, green pastures, so rich and so sweet
God leads His dear children along
Where the water's cool flow bathes the weary one's feet
God leads His dear children along

Some through the waters, some through the flood
Some through the fire, but all through the blood
Some through great sorrow, but God gives a song
In the night season and all the day long[184]

To the many friends and saints of the Most High God,
   It is with a heart full of love and gratitude and thankfulness
that I dedicate this album of songs and trust they may encourage
and strengthen you as we go through the many waters of troubles,
disappointments and trials. It is God's plan to shut us up to faith. Our
circumstances all serve to shut us up and keep us inward 'til we see
that the only way out is God's way of faith.
   Moses tried by self-effort, by personal influence, and even by
violence to bring about the deliverance of God's people. God had to
shut him up forty years in the wilderness before he was prepared for
God's work.

---

184 "God Leads Us Along," by George A. Young, 1903.

Paul and Silas were sent of God to preach the gospel in Europe. They were flogged and they were shut up in prison. Their feet were put fast in the stocks. They were shut up to faith, but they sang praises to Him. In the darkest hour of their trial, God brought deliverance and salvation.

John was banished to the Isle of Patmos. He was shut up, but he had never seen such glorious visions of God. In times of adversity and misunderstandings and trials of all kinds, the Scripture, Isaiah 43:2 has been a comfort to me, and I trust will be to you as it reads like this:

When thou passest through the waters I will be with thee, and through the rivers, they shall not overflow thee. When thou walkest through the fire, thou shall not be burned, neither shall the flame kindle upon thee, for I am the Lord thy God, the Holy one of Israel, thy Savior.[185]

Realizing this is God's plan for His people to purge and to purify, to develop character, to bring them into maturity that He may present unto Himself a glorious church without spot or without wrinkle, many times we cannot understand the road He presents us to travel, but if we trust Him and have faith, we shall see His glory.

Some of the Old Testament prophets God used to teach us these lessons. Abraham could not understand why God asked him to sacrifice his only son. Joseph who could not understand why his brothers hated him, the false witness of an evil woman, and the long years of unjust imprisonment; but he trusted, and he saw at last the glory of God in it all.

And so, perhaps in your life you say, "I do not understand why God let my dear one be taken. I do not understand why affliction has been committed to smite me. I do not understand the strange paths by which the Lord is leading me. I do not understand why plans and purposes that seemed good to my eyes should be baffled. I do not understand why blessings I so much need are so long delayed."

Friend, saints, you do not have to understand all of God's ways with you. God does not expect you to understand Him. You do not expect your child to understand, only believe. Some day, you will

---

185 Isaiah 43:2–3a.

see the glory of God in the things which you do not understand. "Beloved, think it not strange concerning the fiery trial which is to try you as though some strange thing has happened unto you. But rejoice inasmuch as ye are partakers of Christ's sufferings, that when His glory shall be revealed, ye may be glad with exceeding joy."[186]

I have been through the valley of weeping
The valley of sorrow and pain.
But the God of all comfort was with me
—at hand to uphold and sustain.

As the earth needs the clouds and the sunshine,
our souls need both sorrow and joy.
So He places us oft in the furnace,
the dross from the gold to destroy.

When He leads through some valley of trouble,
His omnipotent hand we trace,
for the trials and sorrows He sends us
are part of His lessons in grace.

Oft we shrink from the purging and pruning,
forgetting the husbandman knows
that the deeper the cutting and the pruning,
the richer the cluster grows.

Well He knows that affliction is needed.
He has a wide purpose in view,
and in the dark valley He whispers,
"Hereafter, thou shalt know what I do."

---

186 1 Peter 4:12–13.

As we travel through life's shadowed valley,
fresh springs of His love ever rise
and we learn that our sorrows have lessons.
Losses are blessings, just in disguise.

So we'll follow wherever He leadeth,
let the path be dreary or bright,
for we prove that our God can give comfort,
Our God can give songs in the night.

May God bless every one of you. Be of good courage, is my prayer.

Songs People Remembered Sister Willie Singing

"All Day Long I've Been with Jesus"—Linda McGinnis and Randall Pate

"Down from His Glory"—Nancy Starkey

"Draw Me Closer"—Gracie Mitchell

"God is Still on the Throne"—Neva Limones

"God Leads Us Along"—Linda McGinnis, Brenda Cobbler, Phyllis Asher, Cindy Witt-Means, Deanna Watts, and Elizabeth Lopez

"God's Grace (Greater Than All Our Sin)"—Lois Truman and Charles McCain

"God Rode in a Windstorm"—Margaret Martin, Larry Neal

"He Has Never Left Me Alone" Debby Harrah and Edwin Harper

"He Washed my Eyes with Tears"—Neva Limones, Debby Harrah, and Gene Tatum

"Higher, Higher, Higher—Sandee Huffman

"His Eye is on the Sparrow"—Debby Harrah, Sharri Ballard, and James Stark

"Holding My Savior's Hand"—Kenneth Mendenhall and Shelly Cummings

"I Cannot Fail the Lord"—Neva Limones, Brenda Cobbler, and James Stark

"I Trust in God"—Neva Limones and Debra Dove

"I Won't Go Back"—Larry Neal

"I Won't Have to Cross Jordan Alone"—Larry Neal

"If I Can Just Make it In"—David White

"If I Can Just Touch the Hem of His Garment"—Larry Neal

"I'm in Love with Jesus, and He's in Love with Me"—Marilyn Duhe

"I Won't Come Down"—Sandee Huffman

"Just a Little Touch, Lord, from You"—Donald Haymon

"Just to Behold His Face"—Charlene Barnes

"Keep Holding On"—Pat Forbrush Cohron

"Little Old Wooden Church Way Out on the Hill"—Eileen Willis, Vesta Mangun, Larry Neal

"Lord Lift Me Up and Let Me Stand"—Sandee Huffman

"Love Lifted Me"—Allen Donham

"My Thanks to Him"—Deanna Watts

"Not My Will"—Charlene Barnes

"Oh, Do You Know Him?"—Donald Haymon

"Peace, Peace, Wonderful Peace"—Dan Day

"Remind Me, Dear Lord"—Deanna Watts and James Stark

"Sheltered in the Arms of God"—James Stark

"Since I Met Jesus"—Charlene Barnes

"Submission"—Debby Harrah

"Surely God is Able"—Debby Harrah

"Sweet Holy Spirit"—Gene Tatum

"The Lord Saved Me"—James Stark

"The Lord Will Make a Way Somehow"—Phyllis Asher

"The Love of God"—Shelly Cummings

"Use Me, Oh, Lord"—Deanna Watts and Scottie Chipper Johnson

"We've Come This Far by Faith"—Alice Torres

"When I Met the Master"—Charlene Barnes

"White-Winged Angel"—Larry Neal

"You've Got to Move"—Shelly Cummings, Larry Neal, and William Finn

APPENDIX IV

Sister Willie's Preaching Notes, circa 1967

Preaching Notes from New Castle, Indiana,
c. 1967, picture provided by Larry Neal.

Text: Acts 7:30-34

God never in a hurry. Spends years with those He expects to use greatly.

The hardest ingredient in suffering is time.

Joseph was a long, hard trial.

God has to burn His lessons into the depths of our being. He shall sit as a refiner, a purifier of silver.

He knows how long the moment to see His image.

Let us learn the lessons in the school of sorrow, our deliverer will come.

Genesis 21:2

APPENDIX V

Black History Month
Article by J. Mark Jordan

Sister Willie Johnson was an evangelist in the forties and fifties who had explosive revivals and tent-meetings, many of them here in Ohio. She was known for her Spirit-led ministry and her fearless proclamation of the gospel.

Other prominent black ministers included Samuel Grimes, Bishop Tobin, Bishop Morris Golder, R. C. Lawson, William Bonner, S. N. Hancock, just to name a few. In 2002, the UPCI is home to many outstanding black ministers such as Chester Mitchell, Trevor Neal, F. W. Mckenzie, Will Brewster, Moses Hightower, and Felix Crowder.

As a group, the black component of the early Apostolic movement was disproportionately high. David Bernard says that the majority of the movement was located in three cities, Los Angeles, Oakland, and Indianapolis, and that it was 25–30 percent black. Given the racial climate of the times, this was nothing short of miraculous. S. C. McClain, a white minister from the South, said this:

"I, being Southern born, thought it a miracle that I could sit in a service by a black saint of God and worship, or eat at a great camp table, and forget I was eating beside a black saint, but in spirit and truth God was worshipped in love and harmony.... While all Spirit-filled ministers agreed that with God there is not a color line and in the hearts of the people of God there should be none, yet ministers laboring in the South had to conform to laws and customs." (*A History of Christian Doctrine, Twentieth Century, A. D. 1900–2000*, Volume Three, David Bernard, pp. 94–95.)

In the beginning years, the Southern churches and ministers had not yet come to any conclusions on how to deal with the ironclad racial segregation that was written into many of their state and municipal laws. We do not deny that there were later developments that divided the whites and blacks into separate organizations. At the same time, we must remember that today, in most UPCI churches as well as in most PAW churches, both blacks and whites are welcome and fellowship across racial lines is not an issue whatsoever. The UPCI has a large and growing ministry among African-Americans. The Black Evangelism Conference, a UPCI event sponsored by the Multicultural Ministries of our Home Missions Division, attracts thousands of people every year. Also, our Foreign Missions Division has, for many years, sent missionaries to nations of Africa and other black populations of the world. The greatest influx of souls into the kingdom of God in the past two decades has been from black nations.

The outreach of the church must be universal, without regard to color or race. Tonight, we do emphasize the facts, thoughts and sentiments about our common black heritage in the church in honor of Black History Month. May our overarching goal be to unite, not divide; to show respect, not dishonor; and to work together in the love of God and each other.[187]

---

187 http://jonathanjordan.squarespace.com/local-church-administration/black-history-month.html written in 2007.

Additional Pictures

D.H.S.—Form 2

N. B.—WRITE PLAINLY, WITH UNFADING INK—THIS IS A PERMANENT RECORD. Every item of information should be carefully supplied. AGE should be stated EXACTLY. PHYSICIANS should state CAUSE OF DEATH in plain terms, so that it may be properly classified. Exact statement of OCCUPATION is very important. See instructions on back of certificate.

MARGIN RESERVED FOR BINDING

West Virginia State Department of Health
Division of Vital Statistics

CERTIFICATE OF DEATH

3300

(For State Reg. use only)

1 PLACE OF DEATH (Dist. No. .... No. ....) Series No. ....
(To be inserted by local Registrar)

County ......Marshall......
District .....Washington.....

Town or City ....Moundsville.... No. ....Paine Run.... St., ... Ward
(If death occurred in a hospital or institution, give its name instead of street and number)

2 FULL NAME ....Donald W. Johnson....

(a) Residence. No. .... St., ... Ward. ....
(Usual place of abode)

Length of residence in city or town where death occurred ....yr..... ....mos.....   How long in U. S. A., if of foreign birth? ....yr..... ....mos..... ....days.....
(If nonresident give city or town and state)

PERSONAL AND STATISTICAL PARTICULARS

3 SEX | 4 COLOR OR RACE | 5 Single, Married, Widowed or Divorced (write the word)
Male | Colored White | Single

5a If married, widowed or divorced
HUSBAND of
(or) WIFE of
(Give full maiden name)

6 DATE OF BIRTH ....Nov 26 1928....
(month, day and year)

7 AGE | Years | Months | Days | If LESS than 1 day ....hrs..... ....min.....
| — | 2 | 11 | or

8 OCCUPATION OF DECEASED
(a) Trade, profession or particular kind of work.
(b) General nature of industry, business or establishment in which employed (or employer)
(c) Name of employer

9 BIRTHPLACE (city or town) ....W. Va.....
(State or country)

10 NAME OF FATHER ....Scott Johnson....

11 BIRTHPLACE OF FATHER (city or town) ....Va.....
(State or country)

12 MAIDEN NAME OF MOTHER ....Willia Lane....

13 BIRTHPLACE OF MOTHER (city or town) ....Va.....
(State or country)

14 SIGNATURE OF INFORMANT ....Scott Johnson....
(Address) ....Moundsville....

15 Received ....Feb. 8. 1929. D.B.Daly.... REGISTRAR

MEDICAL CERTIFICATE OF DEATH

16 DATE OF DEATH (Month, day and year) ....Feb..... ....19 29....

17 I HEREBY CERTIFY, That I attended deceased from ....Feb. 5..... 19 29, to ....Feb. 7..... 19 29,
that I last saw h..... alive on ....Feb. 7..... 19 29,
and that death occurred on date stated above, at ....9.25.... M.

The CAUSE OF DEATH was as follows:
(Primary or beginning name)
....Primary Bronchi....
....pneumonia....   (Duration) ....2.... yrs. ....mos. ....da.
....Contributory .grip....
(Secondary or finishing cause)   (Duration) ....mos..... ....da.

18 Where was disease contracted, ...home....
if not at place of death?

Did an operation precede death? ....yes.... Date of ....
Was there an autopsy? ....

What test confirmed diagnosis? ....Bacteriological....
(Signed) ....Wm. G. Thompson.... M. D.
(Address) ....Moundsville....

19 PLACE OF BURIAL ....Grew Lawn....
Cremation or Removal

Date of Burial
Feb. 8 1929

20 Undertaker ....D. C. Lutz....

Address ....Moundsville W. Va.....

MOUNDSVILLE

Donald Johnson death record.

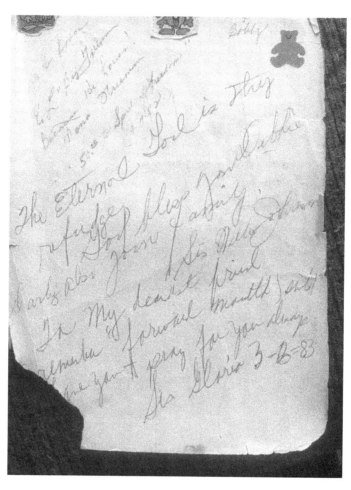

Debbie Kitchen's Bible signed by Sister Willie
and Gloria.

A Note from the Author Regarding Abusive Relationships

In closing Sister Willie's story, I felt it necessary to address the issue of physical abuse. It's impossible for me to speak to all the complexities of her situation, nor am I qualified to do so. Perhaps she hoped to win her unbelieving spouse to the Lord (see 1 Peter 3:1–2). Perhaps she did not feel free in the era or community in which she lived to leave her husband. Or perhaps finances, her children's welfare, or a lack of supportive institutions such as homeless shelters were factors. We don't know the answers to these or other questions, but Sister Willie made it clear by her own words that she felt she should remain true to her wedding vows. Additionally, Sister Willie is on record crediting her suffering for the effectiveness of her ministry that brought healing, deliverance, and hope to others.

We don't know the extent of any injuries Sister Willie sustained. In my opinion, none are acceptable. In fact, one of the most moving moments for me as I researched for this book was when I heard a recording of her singing, "Hold to God's Unchanging Hand." I envisioned her radiant face as she sang the words so many times in services—words that brought joy to herself and so many others. All the while she sang, she knew she would be returning home to the unloving hands of the man who should have been the most tender and kind person in her life. How precious the unchanging hand of God must have been to Willie Johnson.

Whatever Sister Willie's reasons may have been for staying with her husband, she made her choice for herself. If you or someone you know is in a physically abusive relationship, please don't assume Sister Willie's choice to remain in her circumstances is the right choice for you or anyone else.

I want to be clear, I do not believe it is the will of God for one spouse to inflict injury on another. It is not my position that any person should stay in a relationship in which they are being harmed. Every Christian is called to devote himself or herself to others with sincere Christlike affection, even to the point of giving preference to them. The servanthood and love of Christ is most effectively revealed in a godly marriage. Marriage is a picture of the gospel—a husband loves his wife, even as Christ loved the church and gave Himself for it. Men are to love, nourish, and cherish their wives; and wives are to show respect and honor to their husbands. Scripture tells us this is how a Christian marriage is to be, and that it is a mysterious union that speaks of Christ and the church (see Ephesians 5:25–33).

If you or someone you know is in an abusive relationship, help is available. Violence is a crime, and no one deserves to be abused.

Get support. Tell a trusted friend. Contact your pastor, your doctor or nurse, or a social worker. If you feel unsafe, call the police. The National Domestic Violence Hotline can give you the name of a local shelter.

Telephone: 1-800-799-SAFE (7233)

Web site: www.thehotline.org

ADDITIONAL WORKS

BY LORI WAGNER

———————

Ministry Resources
Preach Like a Lady: A Handbook for Women in Ministry
Gender & Ministry: A Biblical and Historical Investigation of Women
*   in Ministry*
Insight on Ministry from a Christmas Tree Farm

Topical Study
Wisdom is a Lady (Small Group Resource Pack)
The Scent of Hope: New Life from Dead Dreams
Holy Intimacy: Dwelling with God in the Secret Place

Fiction
The Briar Hollow Trilogy: *The Rose of Sharon, Buttercup,* and
*   Marigold*
Gateway of the Sun

Discipleship/Christian Growth
Gates & Fences: Straight Talk in a Crooked World
Christian 101: Biblical Basics for New Believers and Youth
The Pure Path Series: *The Girl in the Dress, Covered by Love,*
*   Unmasked,* and *The Pure Life*

Prayer/Devotion

ABC Essentials on a Path of Prayer
Arise! Walk in the Sunrise!
The Eight Days of Christmas

Inspirational

Quilting Patches of Life
A Patchwork of Freedom

Miscellaneous

Bachik, the Birthday Kiss
Pete's Passage
Orbis: The Fun Family Game You Win by Blessing Your World

CPSIA information can be obtained
at www.ICGtesting.com
Printed in the USA
BVHW080246030719
552377BV00031B/1161/P

9 781733 551700